# Parents Who Care Too Much

*B*reaking the cycle
of codependence when a
child's dysfunctional
behavior threatens your
family's sanity & survival

## JAMES M. FARRIS, Ph.D.

*LifeCare*™ Books
from CompCare® Publishers

Library of Congress Cataloging-in-Publication Data
Farris, James M., 1949-
Parents who care too much: breaking the cycle of codependence when a dysfunctional child threatens your family's sanity and survival / James M. Farris
p. cm.
ISBN: 0-89638-275-3
1. Narcotic addicts--Family relationships. 2. Alcoholics--Family relationships. 3. Teenagers--Drug use. 4. Teenagers--Alcohol use. 5. Codependency. 6. Parents of narcotic addicts. 7. Parents of alcoholics. 8. Parenting. I. Title.
RC564.F375  1992
616.8'6--dc20                                                    92-23724
                                                                      CIP

Cover design by Susan Rinek

Inquiries, orders, and catalog requests should be addressed to
CompCare Publishers
2415 Annapolis Lane
Minneapolis, Minnesota 55441
Call toll free 800/328-3330
or 612/559-4800

6     5     4     3     2     1
97    96    95    94    93    92

# Contents

## Part Two:
## Recovering from Parental Codependence

## Part Three:
## Understanding the Adolescent Child

# *Foreword*

As a colleague I watched Dr. James Farris accept the challenge of aiding parents caught between their responsibility for a minor child and their inability to control that child's troubled life. I also observed as he helped parents no longer legally bound to their young adult child, yet aching with grief as their child's life disintegrated. In either case, parental attempts to change the situation too often worsened the problems of addiction and irresponsibility.

Dr. Farris's new work, *Parents Who Care Too Much*, is not really a book to help parents change their grown children. Rather, it is a book to help parents change themselves. Through his study of the attitudes and behaviors of the parents with whom he has worked, Dr. Farris provides insight into a type of codependence not often addressed: parents who do not know when to let go of their child, when to stop trying to change that child's behavior.

But there is a deeper issue discussed in the book. It is the issue of parents' grief when a child doesn't meet their own expectations of a successful, healthy life. Parents must move on from centering themselves on their child to refocusing their lives on themselves. They must ultimately see their child as another person, capable of caring for himself—and needing to face the negative consequences of not doing so. *Parents Who Care Too Much* provides a path for parents to move toward this "letting go" without shame or guilt. It helps parents to further reclaim their own lives as separate human beings, to address their own fears and failures, and once again to find joy in living.

As a colleague and a friend, I congratulate Dr. James Farris on the publication of this book, a summary of many years of service to parents. I hope it will become a resource for others who are working with parents who care too much. Dr. Farris's insights into parenting grown children need to be shared with parents everywhere, parents who are crying out for psychological wholeness and spiritual health.

—Jack Felton

# Introduction
# The Child I Love—The
# Child I Hate

*I just don't know what to do. I want to hit him and scream at him. But he is the same boy that I loved and held and played with. Please help me. I don't have any more ideas and I am too tired to try to help him anymore.*

—Jerry's father

J erry had been a problem for his parents since he was fourteen years old. Eventually, at the age of twenty-one, he had disappeared from his family—at least temporarily. At that point Jerry's worried parents came to me seeking help to deal with their son, his addictions, and his destructive behavior.

Jerry's troubles began when, as a fourteen-year-old freshman, he started skipping classes at his large high school in southern California. Previous to his first year in high school, Jerry had been an above-average student. He earned B and C grades in most classes, participated in some sports, and had a few friends with whom he spent time going to the beach or just "hanging around."

Jerry's parents first noticed changes in their son's life when a school official called about Jerry's numerous absences. The official was concerned that Jerry's mother had written so many notes to excuse the boy's absences yet had not responded to notes sent home about Jerry's not making up work he had missed when absent.

With this evidence in hand, the parents confronted Jerry about his absences and the obviously forged notes. However, nothing changed. Jerry seemed apologetic, but he soon resumed the behavior and became argumentative and defensive about his absences.

By age fifteen Jerry was missing school most of the time, so his parents made a deal with him: they would buy him a guitar if he would promise to attend school regularly. The promise lasted one week. Jerry's father got so angry with him that they had a fistfight. Jerry then left home for six days.

At sixteen Jerry's parents bought him a car because he promised to stay in a continuation school. This promise lasted a month. They then decided to send Jerry to live with his uncle in a small Colorado town. Jerry lived there for three months, then returned after destroying the uncle's car.

When Jerry returned he begged to quit school and find a job. His parents relented. He landed a job in a deli, then quit and secured another job in a bicycle shop. By age seventeen he had gone through two more jobs, and finally he left home.

Four years later, by the time his parents had come to see me, Jerry had demolished five cars and had been arrested in five states for possession of drugs or driving under the influence of alcohol. He also had been arrested in Canada for theft, although the charges were dropped when his parents agreed to pay for the things he had stolen.

Over the years his parents had spent more than $60,000 to bail him out of jail or pay for damages he caused in numerous locations. Although both spouses were making good incomes, they lived in a two-bedroom apartment because they could not afford to buy a house—they were spending all of their money on Jerry.

## The forgotten sibling

Almost forgotten amid the rubble of Jerry's life was his younger brother Jimmy. Actually, he was the original reason for my meeting Jerry's family. Afraid that Jimmy would become another Jerry, they brought Jimmy to see me when his grades began dropping to the D and F level. Sadly, and ironically, Jimmy was doing the exact opposite of his brother Jerry—he was destroying *himself* rather than those around him.

During our second interview Jimmy exposed his deep, seething anger toward Jerry and his parents. It was an anger I have witnessed in dozens of families where parents have lost their perspective as they care too much for a child exhibiting dysfunctional behavior and thus neglect other children—and themselves.

The tragedy of Jerry's family is the story that convinced me to write this book. Jerry's story, however, is only one of many I have heard from parents of children, both adolescents and young adults, who are addicted to drugs or exhibit dysfunctional behavior. Though it may appear an extreme account of pain and disappointment in a family, it is quite typical of such stories: parents who give everything to change their child's behavior and thus jeopardize the whole family; parents who plead with, bargain with, and threaten their child in trying to stop the child's destructive behavior.

The loser in such a story is not just the adolescent or young adult who is destroying her life, but every member of such a family. Parents are agonized with guilt and self-recrimination, asking themselves where they have gone wrong and fearing for the future. Siblings of the dysfunctionally behaving child feel neglected as they watch the problem child receiving all of the attention for bad behavior. Teachers, counselors, and well-meaning relatives as well are at their wits' end in attempting to help the parents of such a troubled child.

Yet there is hope for such a family. And because you, a frustrated parent, are reading this book I believe that you also believe hope can be found. But before we proceed together, please allow a brief explanation of the teenage years (whether that child of yours is now a teenager or an adult) that will help you understand what has happened inside that child.

# Understanding the tumultuous years

The teenage years are difficult for almost everyone because, during this time, adolescents realize that they are no longer children but not yet adults. They begin to learn the responsibilities of adulthood as they leave the comfort of childhood. They also learn that responsibility means facing the consequences of their actions. This, perhaps, is the ultimate role of adolescence. Once the role is completed the adolescent crosses an invisible threshold into adulthood.

Completing this task, of course, is not a one-time activity, but many small steps of accepting responsibility. This usually culminates in the child becoming a responsible adult.

But, you may argue, there are many irresponsible adults. I agree. Such adults have not completed the task of maturation—which is the precise reason I have written this book: *parents do not help their child mature if they, by providing artificial supports, prevent that child from completing the steps that lead to responsible adulthood.*

The teenage years are difficult for the parents, too, because it means they must let go of their adolescent child. They must allow the child more and more freedom, or else she will seize freedom through conflict with parents and all other social authority figures (unless the child chooses to be despondent and fearful and thus hide behind parental authority).

# Learning to let go

Permitting more freedom is difficult for parents for two reasons. First, parents are afraid their child will be hurt physically or emotionally in ways that may last forever, or at least for a large part of that child's adult life. And second, parents realize their grown child no longer needs them (in the same way). As parents, therefore, they are being catapulted into a new phase of adult life. This change may be difficult to accept because it means an "empty nest" and eventual grandparenthood.

In facing these challenges the greatest virtues for parents of an adolescent or adult child are *courage* and *a sense of balance.* This book is intended to help you quicken those virtues in your life—to find the courage to love your son or daughter in a way that begins restoration, and to maintain the balance that will bring that restoration to its fullness.

I also hope that the parents of the "Jerrys" of our society, and parents with less-troubled youth, will benefit from these writings by realizing their limitations; by sharing the journey with other parents who travel the same difficult road; and by learning to deal with hard situations by making a step-by-step plan—and courageously admitting their shortcomings and failures when they do otherwise. That is the way to recovery from parental codependence.

—James M. Farris, Ph.D.
*Laguna Beach, California*

## "A Parent's Prayer"

*O God,*
*Grant me serenity to accept circumstances*
*in my child's life which I cannot change—*
*which can only be changed by my child. Grant me also*
*the serenity to accept circumstances*
*in my child's life which cannot be changed at all—*
*neither by me nor by my child.*

*Grant me courage to influence and change my child's*
*life for the better—but only in the ways and areas*
*appropriate for me to change.*

*Grant me also the courage to stand aside when others*
*must be the ones to change my child's life—others who*
*perhaps have yet to touch*
*my child's life.*

*Grant me, finally, the wisdom to know the difference*
*between helping and holding on; between loving and*
*controlling out of fear; between addressing my child's*
*needs*
*and my own needs.*

*Amen*

## PART ONE

# Recognizing Parental Codependence

# "Your Family Is Dying": The Story of Marcie's Family

---

*What has happened to our family? In a short time everything has changed and I don't recognize us any more. We've all changed. We're so far apart.*

—Marcie's mother

---

I had just finished a talk on setting limits as a parent of adolescents when Ray stepped up to me with desperation taut on his face.

"It's about our daughter, Marcie," Ray said. "Could my wife and I have an appointment with you?" He had come to the conference on codependent parents because Marcie, seventeen, had been through three treatment programs in two years. He and his wife, June, had run out of answers to the problem.

"I'd like to see the whole family—except Marcie, of course," I replied. Though surprised at my request to exclude Marcie, he agreed, and a few days later we met in my office.

Present at that first meeting were Ray, June, and Marcie's two younger siblings, Cindy and Mark, ages twelve and fifteen. An older daughter lived in Arizona. Our first session proceeded as follows.

**Ray:** *I hope you can help Marcie. We haven't been able to get any real help for her. She's still using drugs.*

**June:** *We've tried three different hospital programs and Marcie ran away from two of them. She liked one program and stayed there for a month. After that program she stopped using drugs for at least a month.*

The two children sat self-conscious and restless—and silent. After about ten minutes of conversation with the parents I turned to Cindy and Mark and asked them a question.

**Farris:** *What about you two? What do you think about this Marcie business?*

**Cindy:** *Nothing.*

**Farris:** *And what about you, Mark? You must have an opinion about the relationship between Marcie and the rest of the family.*

**Mark:** *I don't know.*

**Farris:** *I don't believe either of you. I'd bet you're thinking, "I am so tired of hearing Marcie's name. That's all they talk about— Marcie, Marcie, Marcie! I'm sick of it."*

**Cindy:** *Yeah, and we can't do anything because of Marcie. We couldn't go to Disney World last summer because of Marcie—* (turning to her parents) *and you promised!*

**Farris:** *Mark, you may as well speak now. You may never get another chance to say what you really think about this Marcie business and how it's affecting your family.*

**Mark:** *I'm tired of it. I couldn't even go to the beach last Saturday because of her. While you* (looking at his mother) *and Dad went to that wedding, I had to stay at home just in case Marcie was using drugs.*

**Ray:** *It has been hard on the other kids. We had to stay at home last summer because we were afraid that if we left, Marcie would just have a field day with drugs. I'm sorry, kids, that it happened that way.*

**Farris:** *So, staying at home keeps Marcie from using drugs.*

**June:** *No. She still uses them—but we don't allow it at home. We don't want her influencing Mark and Cindy.*

**Farris:** *I think she's already influencing Mark and Cindy. Their lives have a big dent because of the family's concern for Marcie.*

**June:** *But Marcie would bring the drugs into the house if we didn't watch her. That's why we're here—to control her drugs so that we can go back to normal.*

**Farris:** *I have a different suggestion. Go back to normal first.*

**Ray:** *What do you mean? If we could do that, we wouldn't be here.*

**Farris:** *I think you need to work on your family, not on Marcie. Your family life is almost dead. Your younger children have disrupted lives, and I'd bet your marriage is in bad shape. All your attention is on Marcie, so you have no time for any other relationship.*

**June:** *But if we can stop Marcie from using drugs, we could go back to being a normal family.*

**Farris:** *I don't think so. If Marcie stopped using drugs, you would fall apart as a family. That's the only thing that you do together as a family anymore: talk about Marcie.*

**June:** *But we all love Marcie. That's why we're here—to help her. We are her family and we want to help—*

**Mark:** *I don't love her. I'm sick of her, and I'm sick of talking about her. "Marcie, Marcie, Marcie." That's all we hear.*

**Ray:** *Mark, that's not fair!*

**Cindy:** *We couldn't even have Grandma and Grandpa over last Christmas because of Marcie.*

**June:** *But Marcie made such a scene at Thanksgiving—we were so embarrassed. Just before dinner she learned I had searched her drawer that morning to make sure she wasn't hiding drugs. She threw a screaming fit. I didn't want a repeat of that scene, so we had Christmas dinner just for our family.*

**Farris:** *So everyone suffered because of Marcie. Why do you want to keep suffering?*

**Ray:** *That's why we're here, so you can help us with Marcie's drug problem.*

**Farris:** *I see a more important problem. Your family is dying. I can't help you with Marcie's problem until I can help your family first. Are you willing to work on that first, as a family?*

**Ray:** *Well, however you see it.*

**June:** *But we can't just drop Marcie. That's why we're here.*

**Farris:** *June, these children are suffering, not just Marcie. They feel neglected. Your husband feels neglected. You feel neglected. Can you see that your relationships with each other are dying because all the attention is on Marcie?*

**June:** *But there's only one me!* (She begins to weep.) *I can't do it all. I don't know what to do anymore. There's Marcie, using drugs all the time. I can't split myself. Mark and Cindy don't have a drug problem, Marcie does.*

**Farris:** *But Mark and Cindy have other problems, and other needs. And you have needs, and so does Ray. Each of you needs time and attention, but all the time and attention is going to Marcie. I can help you, but you each have to commit to working on yourselves first, as individuals and as a family. Do you understand? And do you agree?*

**Ray:** *Well, I think I understand, and I'll go along with it. But you'll have to explain more about how this can help Marcie.*

**Farris:** *Easy! You can't help Marcie until you are healthy as a family. And believe me, you are not healthy now. Do you feel that?*

**Ray:** (Hanging his head): *Yes.*

**Mark:** *I understand.*

**Cindy:** *So do I.*

**June:** *I'm sorry, but I don't. We came here because Marcie is using drugs, and instead you're telling us we are the sick ones.*

**Farris:** *And I can prove it. No vacation, no Christmas, no beach for Mark. All of you are living for Marcie. Is that healthy or sick?*

**Mark:** *Sick!*

**Farris:** *June, you love your children and your husband. Please trust me when I say you must work on the family first. Are you willing to do at least that much? If you are, you'll understand* *what I mean as we continue the family sessions. Can you do at least that much?*

**June:** *Well, I'm still not sure, but I'll go along with what you say. I guess that's why we came—to get your help.*

**Farris:** *And I promise that if you follow my advice, you'll be helped. Believe me. So let's start by talking more about how family life was before Marcie started using drugs. . . .*

The story of Marcie's family is common among families with a drug-abusing child. It is the story of codependence in which everyone suffers because of the drug abuse as the family slowly disintegrates through anger and exhaustion. Rather than curing the drug user's problem, codependence creates more problems for the whole family.

# *Reflections*

*There is no fear in love, but perfect love casts out fear. For fear has to do with punishment, and he who fears is not perfected in love.*

—1 John 4:18

1. What is the most fearful thing about your family's situation? How often do you worry about it?

2. Do you remember fear in your family when you were a child? What were you afraid of as a child?

# Older, But not Wiser: The Story of Kenney's Family

*I wish I could take his place and die for him.*
*Why is he like this?*

—Norma, mother of a forty-year-old drug addict

## A story of attempted love

Norma and Jack had four children. The two oldest and the youngest grew up with the usual difficulties but were considered by Norma and Jack to be successful people: all were now married and had produced five grandchildren.

The child who caused Norma and Jack worry was their third, a son named Kenney. He always seemed to have problems when going through school and was often in trouble with authorities. This was a special embarrassment for Jack, a school principal. Jack felt ashamed that Kenney was so troublesome in the same school system in which which his father worked.

When Kenney graduated from high school Jack and Norma felt great relief. With Kenney now out of the house and responsible for himself, their troubles would finally be over. Wrong. They slowly discovered themselves to be voluntary victims, poised for a lifetime of anxiety in their codependent relationship with Kenney.

At nineteen years old Kenney was arrested for the first time, for possessing cocaine and driving under the influence of alcohol. He called his parents. They came immediately, paid his bail, and found him an attorney. At the hearing Kenney promised to go to a hospital for treatment, and because this was Kenney's first offense, the judge granted a light sentence in response to the young man's apparent sincerity.

Wanting to help Kenney, Norma and Jack let him stay at home until he found a job. Two weeks after the sentencing, however, Norma found cocaine in Kenney's room. As the years progressed Kenney's life became a pattern of temporary jobs, drugs, treatment programs, promises of reform, then relapses into drug use.

Jack died when Kenney was thirty-six years old. Jack left enough money, property, and stocks for Norma to live very comfortably; he also left a large insurance policy that benefitted Norma and gave some money to each child. However, the money did not provide Norma a happy life.

Norma came to see me four years after Jack's death. She was now sixty-eight years old and had a part-time job at a florist shop. She enjoyed her work, but thanks to Kenney, the rest of her life was pure misery.

## Dreading her own child's voice

Norma related how she and Jack had spent thousands of dollars on Kenney during the last twenty years. They had bailed him out of jail, sent him money to live in a apartment, and put him in programs to help him get sober. Nothing had worked. Now Norma sat next to her phone each night, terrified that Kenney would call to ask her for more money. He always had a good excuse. Here is how Norma finally realized the severity of her codependent behavior:

**Norma:** *Kenney called from Arizona last week—said he'd lost his job. He told me the manager of the gas station where he was working accused him of stealing money. He swore to me that he didn't do it. I sent him enough money to pay his rent for next month. When he came out of the bank after cashing my money order, two men jumped him, hit him with a pipe, and took the money. He was bleeding so badly he had to go to an emergency room. So I* *had to send him more money so he could pay the hospital for treating his injuries.*

**Farris:** *And, of course, you sent him more money to cover the rent, because the original money had been stolen.*

**Norma:** *What could I do? He was bleeding! He needed the money. I couldn't just leave him on the street.*

**Farris:** *Norma, let's look at how much you have been spending on Kenney, just in the last four years since Jack died.*

**Norma:** *Oh, I can't. I know it's so much. Jack would be horrified.*

**Farris:** *From what you have been telling me, I guess you've been spending about twenty thousand dollars a year on drugs for Kenney.*

**Norma:** *No! No! Not on drugs! I've been sending him money to live. He's spending his own money on the drugs—and I don't know how to get him to stop.*

**Farris:** *The money you send him allows him to live and the money he earns goes to drugs. Did it ever occur to you that every dollar you send him helps him to live as a drug addict? Face it, you are helping him to use drugs. Why should he want to quit? He has it made. He doesn't have to work; he can just use drugs and take money from you.*

**Norma:** *But what can I do? He needs to live.*

**Farris:** *At this rate, he's not going to live. The drugs are taking him to sure death. He's on a suicide path.*

**Norma:** (She begins to cry.): *But what can I do? I gave him the money from his father's insurance policy and he spent it in a few months. He's our son. He's always had a problem, and I think Jack and I may have been the cause. We didn't give him as much time as we should have because his sister was born so soon after his birth. I wish I could take his place and die for him. Why is he like this?*

**Farris:** *I don't know why he is like this. However, I do know why he stays like this. You are helping him to do so. The cause of his addiction is one thing. The maintenance of his addiction is another. If you want to help him, you must take small steps and follow* *my directions. You must also ask your family to come in with you. You can't help Kenney until you help yourself. You are codependent—you must find out how to change yourself.*

*You can never change Kenney. You haven't done so for forty years. Only Kenney can change himself by choosing a program of recovery. That is not your decision, it's Kenney's. But you can make a decision to help yourself—and to help Kenney by helping yourself. You can stop supplying his drug money.*

**Norma:** *I want to do it, but I'm afraid. Every time he calls, I just give in to him. He sounds so pitiful. He's trying so hard, but he just can't do it.*

**Farris:** *Norma, Kenney will die soon if he continues this drug life. Do you want to be a part of his death? Or would you rather be a loved one waiting for him to choose life?*

**Norma:** *I want to help him.*

**Farris:** *Then stop giving him drug money.*

**Norma:** *What do I do when he calls?*

**Farris:** *Buy an answering machine to take all your calls; then you can review them to choose the calls you want to return. That can be step one. After that, we'll take other steps. Are you willing?*

**Norma:** *Yes, but I'm afraid.*

**Farris:** *Fear is not a problem. You can be afraid and trust at the same time.*

**Norma:** *Then I'm willing.*

**Farris:** *Good. At the next session I want as many of your children as possible to come with you—with the exception of Kenney. Do you think that, at least, one or two can come for the next session?*

**Norma:** *I'll ask. I think two can come, but one of my daughters lives too far away.*

**Farris:** *Two out of three will be very good. Let's take it a step at a time—and remember, we're working on helping you out of this terrible state of anxiety. I have a plan that will work if you'll cooperate. Do you understand?*

**Norma:** *Yes. And thank you. I already feel better—I feel as if there's hope.*

During the next twenty months Norma gradually broke free from her codependent habits. She attended workshops, self-help groups, and therapy sessions. And with the help of her family and many others, she stopped her self-destructive style of life.

As Norma and I worked together I learned how destructive that lifestyle could be; it had killed her husband, Jack. Norma told me that while Kenney was home again—for the fifth time—he had stolen money from his parents. Jack's health, already fragile, could not withstand another shock. The incident raised his anxiety to an intolerable level, and several days later he died.

As Norma and I discussed this she realized that we were saving her from a similar fate—one not uncommon for codependents. We were saving her life.

# *Reflections*

---

*If any one will not work, let him not eat.*

—2 Thessalonians 3:10

---

1. Are you supporting an adult son or daughter who will not work or who is not sincerely trying to find work? In what ways are you doing this?

2. Are you supporting an adult son or daughter who is working but spends money on alcohol and drugs or in other irresponsible ways? How are you justifying this support?

# Understanding Codependence

*Some of us veered from extreme to extreme
ever hoping that one day our loved ones would be
themselves once more.*

—The "Big Book" of Alcoholics Anonymous (p. 105)

The stories of Ray and June and of Jack and Norma are stories of codependence. They are stories of people sharing the pain of a family system that results in sickness. Nonetheless, that system is sustained because its members feel trapped, with no alternatives. Though it gives them pain, it is a pain they know—a pain less scary than the pain of choosing new alternatives. The pain may be familiar to you.

## A mirror for codependence

The following description of codependence is meant to be a mirror that can help a person identify codependent behavior. By looking into this description they can know whether or not they might be living in the style of a codependent.

**Definition: Codependence is living within a system in which one person takes responsibility for another who is acting irresponsibly and destroying his or her own life.**

Whether the relationship is spouse and spouse, child and parent, or friend and friend, a codependent inappropriately takes on responsibility for another person. It is an attempt to control something that the codependent never will be able to control, whether the problem be alcohol, drugs, sexual behavior, eating, or some other compulsive behavior.

By focusing this intently on others' behavior, codependents are no longer aware of their own compulsive and addictive behaviors. This obsession leads to loss of control over their own lives.

## Codependents cannot identify personal feelings

Such persons probably are confused and numb. They have repressed feelings that are too painful and too glaringly honest to admit. With the loss of these feelings goes the loss of other feelings as well. Joy, as well as sorrow, is suppressed. Anger and serenity, contentment and grief are all pushed away from consciousness. This is an attempt to deny a problem by not facing it.

## Codependents feel guilty about failing to meet responsibilities because those responsibilities are overwhelming

Usually one of the feelings codependents allow is guilt—and they feel it often. They probably will feel guilty about the actions of the dependent/addicted person with whom they are involved. The common, though false, belief is stated this way: "I have caused this person to drink (or use drugs, or overeat, et cetera)." The codependent also is likely to feel a high degree of perfectionism, expecting too much of both themselves and others—for example, "Why can't the doctor stop my son from using drugs?"

## Codependents usually have an area of life that contradicts perfectionism

This may be a glaring addiction or a hidden problem. If it is an addiction, it is always different from the addiction of the person with whom they are codependent. A codependent may be an alcoholic but complain about the drug use of the dysfunctionally behaving child. The codependent may be a compulsive overeater but complain about an alcoholic spouse. In many cases, however, the loss of control is hidden, such as secret sexual behavior.

Whatever it is, the codependent lives in complete denial of the fault.

## Codependents cannot openly express thoughts and feelings

Codependents may fear the consequences of expressing themselves. They therefore cannot tell the addicted dependent in their life the truth about pain in the relationship or about their own secret addictions. Fear that the dependent person will no longer love or need them can paralyze expression of personal feelings.

## Codependents are stuck in patterns of life that simply do not work

They may have difficulty making changes in their lives, often feeling powerless over themselves, constantly feeling victimized in many areas of life. They also may feel shame over perceived failures that *seem* unrelated to codependence (such as their own addiction to food, alcohol, or tobacco).

## Codependents want to be close to others, but they avoid the risk for fear of being hurt

Sometimes this may be emotional fatigue—feeling too tired to attempt being close to others. Their ties to others are never well established because of ambiguous feelings toward each person in their lives. They may alternately feel close and critical about every relationship they have. Finally the person will give up—"I just don't fit in."

# Marks of a codependent parent

## Codependent parents feel super-responsible for the behavior of each child

A typical statement I hear from codependent parents is, "If only I were a better parent, my child could have grown up more successful, more talented, more educated, more . . ." Parents can easily believe themselves to be in a supreme position of influencing their child's life, even if that child is grown. Such parents will find it difficult, even impossible, to accept a child—with both virtues and faults—unconditionally.

## Codependent parents have a constant need for the approval of others

Such parents wants others to understand how difficult the situation is and how much suffering occurs. They want sympathy for "martyrdom" but feel insulted when someone suggests they could stop being a martyr by stopping their codependent behavior.

## Codependent parents are deeply embarrassed by the behavior of an addicted or dysfunctionally behaving child

They feel judged by others because of the way their child acts. They want to be proper and acceptable and want the child to be that way, too. The behavior of the addicted child brings more shame than grief because these parents want approval, not only for their own behavior, but also for the behavior of their child. They thus will exaggerate the accomplishments of a "good" child to gain this acceptability.

# Am I a codependent parent?

The following questionnaire should be helpful in identifying codependent behavior. Answer the questions as honestly as is possible. Don't be too harsh or too easy on yourself. Remember that although the questions speak about your "child," they are about your child who is now adult, or nearly so. Your answers will reveal much about your relationship with that person who is your son or daughter.

1. Does my child undergo personality changes after drinking in excess? ❑ Yes ❑ No

2. Have I seen other changes, for no apparent reason, in my child's behavior? ❑ Yes ❑ No

3. Do I feel that alcohol or other drugs are more important to my child than I am or my family is? ❑ Yes ❑ No

4. Because of my child's addictive behavior do I feel self-pity and often think, "I wish things were different with her so we all would be happy"? ❑ Yes ❑ No

5. As a result of his use of drugs or alcohol, have I supported

my child by supplying money, a home, or care for his child, or by paying bail?    ❑ Yes    ❑ No

6.  Does my child's drinking or use of drugs cause arguments in the family?    ❑ Yes    ❑ No

7.  Am I angry or depressed about this alcohol or drug use?
    ❑ Yes    ❑ No

8.  Have I felt guilty or apologetic about this alcohol or drug use (or expressed embarrassment to others because of it)?
    ❑ Yes    ❑ No

9.  Have I tried to stop or control my child's use of drugs or alcohol by hiding liquor, fighting over the car keys, or taking over responsibility of my child's spending money?
    ❑ Yes    ❑ No

10.  Do I often worry about my child's use of alcohol and drugs? Has it made my home an unhappy place to live?
    ❑ Yes    ❑ No

11.  Are family gatherings difficult because of my child's use of alcohol or drugs and her related behavior?    ❑ Yes    ❑ No

12.  Has my child made repeated—and broken—promises to stop alcohol or drug use?    ❑ Yes    ❑ No

13.  Do other members of my family have difficulty with the use of alcohol, drugs, or prescribed medication?
    ❑ Yes    ❑ No

14.  Do my plans hinge on my child's schedule (in order to take responsibility for my child's affairs)?    ❑ Yes    ❑ No

15.  Do I avoid social situations because I am embarrassed by my child's drinking or drug use? Do I refrain from having friends at my home when my child is there because of fear that the child's behavior might embarrass me?    ❑ Yes    ❑ No

16.  Has my drinking, use of drugs, or use of medication increased because of my child's behavior?    ❑ Yes    ❑ No

17.  Am I afraid to give my child responsibilities, for fear of the results?    ❑ Yes    ❑ No

Now tally your yes answers. If you answered even three or four with a yes, it's time to take a hard look at what probably is codependent behavior.

# Codependent parents of a dysfunctionally behaving adult

Although codependence toward any loved one reveals common characteristics, the experience of a parent with a dysfunctionally behaving adult child is nonetheless unique. The thoughts of codependent parents of adults who act dysfunctionally, especially because of the use of alcohol or drugs, are often expressed in the following ways:

## Denial

"I can't believe this has happened to me." [If married to an addicted person, they have sworn never to let this happen to their kids. And if personally addicted, they find it unbelievable that their child now faces the same pain.]

## Anger

"I'm angry that my child turned out like this. My trust in my child has been broken. I'm angry at life—even God—for having saddled me with this problem." [This problem may be compounded if either parent is also addicted.]

## Protectiveness

"Day by day I've been faithfully defending my child from the consequences of the cruel world. Life seems so unjust; my child feels cheated out of his life goals (job, spouse, family, home, and so forth). I must side with my child against the world, and I must feel sorry for him—that's a parent's duty!"

## Guilt

"I am to blame for my child's behavior. If only I were a better parent. I guess I didn't give my child enough time (or money, attention, et cetera). I must make up for it now by helping bear the difficulties in her life." [If parents are addicted or recovering from addiction, their guilt doubles when they recall periods when they, because of addiction, have failed as a parent.]

## Anxiety

"I worry constantly about my child. I seem to have lost my own life and my own concerns as I've focused more and more on the behavior of my child. I now worry about his job, schedule, friends, and other aspects of my child's life."

## Disappointment and embarrassment

"I think about what my child might be if only she were not chemically addicted, if only she had her life 'together.' I fantasize about my child being normal, and I want to believe that this time things will be different. I avoid situations and people who know my child and who may judge me because of my child. I'm embarrassed about my child's behavior and feel shame. I even avoid family gatherings that may include my child, because I'm afraid of her actions."

# *Reflections*

*We have traveled a rocky road, there is no mistake about that. We have had long rendezvous with hurt pride, frustration, self-pity, misunderstanding and fear. These are not pleasant companions.*

—The "Big Book" of Alcoholics Anonymous (p. 104)

1. Make a list of all family members and friends who have been affected by your child's dysfunctional behavior.

2. How do you feel after reading the list?

3. If you are the parent of a dysfunctional person, is your child's behavior a reflection of part of your life? If so, in what ways is your child's behavior different from yours?

# 4

# *The Stages of Codependence: A Parallel Illness*

---

*Let us not think that everything is accomplished through much weeping, but set our hands to the task of hard work and virtue.*

—Teresa of Avila, The Interior Castle

---

Codependence can be as devastating as addiction to drugs or alcohol. First, like addiction, codependence affects the individual's mental health as well as his physical health, because of the stress caused by codependent behavior. Next, like addiction, codependence has a progression through distinct stages. This chapter will trace its progression to its most debilitating state of physical or emotional illness. Finally, and most heartening, like addiction codependence can be treated and the codependent can recover.

## Stage one: moderate codependent behaviors and attitudes

This is the first stage of parental codependence. Parents in this stage have experienced, though moderately, the debilitating effects of the way they live. Too often at this stage they do not recognize the reality of codependence.

If they do recognize it, they fear rocking the family "boat" by doing something to correct the problem. They also fear that other family members will reproach them or that their other children will no longer love them.

## 1. A loss of daily structure to care for the child's needs

Codependent parents change plans with friends and other family members because of the needs of the child, even if that child is an adult. Although that child may be capable of handling his own personal affairs, the parent takes responsibility and control of the child's life by this codependent behavior—doing things that the child could do.

## 2. Decreased care for personal appearance and health

Parents change even healthy parts of their schedule to take care of the affairs of the child. They may gain weight, neglect make-up or hair cuts, or stop exercising. They do this under the pretext of not having enough time because of the demands of caring for the needs of the dysfunctionally behaving child.

## 3. Inability to set limits for the child who behaves in a dysfunctional manner

Limit setting means refusing to do for the child what she should do for herself. When this breaks down, parents allow the child to continually ask for money—and receive it. If an adult, the child may increasingly borrow items from the parents' house and impose on parents to baby-sit while on a drug or alcohol binge. The parents do more and more for the child without any sense of reciprocation; they allow the use of themselves, their home, and their possessions, yet demand nothing in return.

## 4. Increased difficulty in making decisions

Codependent parents have to make decisions that leave them caught between both sides of those decisions (such as asking an adult child not to take food from the parents' refrigerator while realizing that the child's own children are without food). Crippled by such dilemmas, the parents' growing inability to make decisions spills over into their everyday decisions. Their depression and anxiety create cloudy and confused thinking, and issues become increasingly unclear.

## 5. Compulsive behaviors

Codependent parents begin to exhibit an increasing amount of compulsive behavior, such as greater use of alcohol or tobacco. This compulsive style becomes a part of everyday life as the parent tries to escape anxiety through compulsive buying or through sexual and other compulsive deviations from normal behavior. These actions reveal an attempt to distract themselves from the distress of codependence.

## 6. Fatigue and inability to rest

These parents worry increasingly about the future—that is, "Where will all this lead?" They are troubled about the money they are spending to help the dysfunctionally acting child; the responsibility for the grandchildren (if the child is also a parent); and the neglect of their own needs and desires. They are exhausted from caring for both themselves and their child as they try to control the child's life. And they find that their own lives are out of control.

## 7. Increased resentment and unfocused anger

Codependent parents feel angry all the time, but the anger is revealed unpredictably. Often it is set off by a small matter rather than the true reason for the anger—the codependent relationship with their child. There appears to be no particular reason for the constant resentment. The parent feels always on edge, but when asked about all that they do for the dysfunctionally behaving child, especially if the child is an adult, they simply respond that they feel obligated to help.

## 8. Self-pity and compensation through self-indulgence

Feeling sorry for themselves, codependent parents begin to reward themselves in nonhealthy ways—overeating as a reward for suffering, or drinking to excess because "I deserve it after the difficult argument I had today with my child." Such parents may even feel the need to justify normal behavior by turning it into indulgence thinking (for instance, "I deserve a new suit because my life is so tough").

### 9. Blaming others for problems

Exhausted from the burden of caring for their child's life, these parents begin to seek other outlets for anger rather than holding the child responsible. They thus start to blame others for their problems, especially the child's problems ("Those stupid teachers at the high school caused all this because they gave Sara such a terrible education").

# Stage two: severe codependent behaviors and attitudes

The second stage is marked by severe codependence as the deterioration of the parents' mental and physical health becomes increasingly apparent. Old patterns of dysfunction become more ingrained in the parents' lives. They feel the dilemma is fixed, that the situation is hopeless. Despite the increase in crises—which should be opportunities to break out of the cycle, their denial of the problem persists.

### 10. Obsession with past failures and generalized anxiety

Codependent parents begin to scrutinize their lives and find every seeming failure they have experienced as a person and as a parent. They ruminate greatly on the failures connected with the child who is now addicted. The sense of hopelessness increases and the parents begin to ask questions about the meaning of their lives.

### 11. Breakdown of the spiritual system

"Why is this happening to me?" or "Why has God abandoned me?" is a typical question voiced by codependent parents as hope continues to fade from their dysfunctional system. God seems distant, prayer and meditation feel impossible, and serenity and comfort from the practice of their faith are gone.

### 12. Confused thinking and overwhelming thoughts

Depression and anxiety increase. Racing thoughts begin to hamper their ability to think clearly. Worry over their child dominates their consciousness, distracting them from work or conversations with family and friends. They become obsessed with seemingly inconsequential matters in their attempt to gain control over life's activities.

## 13. Sleep disturbances and mood swings

Anxiety leaves them unable to sleep—obsessive thoughts intrude on their ability to relax. They worry until exhausted and irritable. Getting though the day grows more difficult because they sleep little at night. Depression follows exhaustion. When the child finds a job, promises to stop using drugs, or takes some other positive step, parents feel revived by hope—but when the hope turns sour they again sink into depression.

## 14. Withdrawal from others to focus on family problems

Friendships wither away. Codependent parents no longer have time to spend on friends, hobbies, or interests. Any responsibilities they have assumed for the child, and the ensuing worry about that child, consume their time, attention, and energy. Often this consumes the parents' money as well, leaving little to spend on their own needs and desires.

## 15. Refusal of aid from professionals or self-help groups

Codependent parents feel too tired to attend any meetings or therapy sessions. They excuse themselves with "I just don't have the energy to go." If they do go, however, they may conclude, "I don't feel as if I fit in. I'm different from those people at the self-help group. My life isn't like that. My child isn't that bad." Therapists, also, "just don't understand." Typically the parent is dissatisfied because the cure isn't instant or magically easy.

## 16. Health problems, such as hypertension, stomach ulcer, arthritis, muscle pain

The classic health problems associated with stress now appear. In such cases high blood pressure, a symptom of tension, is common. Such health problems are exacerbated by increased smoking or drinking or by eating compulsions. Weight loss or gain will likely continue as stress increases. This prolonged stress lowers immunity to colds, flu, and other sicknesses.

### 17. Attempted relaxation using alcohol, drugs, and prescribed medication

Inability to relax and sleep, combined with constant anxiety, will lead parents to seek help through medication prescribed by a physician. As an alternative they may self-medicate with alcohol or illegal drugs. For some codependent parents, this may be their first experience with addictive substances. Whether this is a new or increased use of narcotics, these parents heighten their sense of guilt and confusion.

## Stage three: extreme codependent behaviors and attitudes

The third stage of codependence is termed "extreme" because it is life threatening. As life seemingly grows ever more hopeless, codependent parents grow ever more desperate. They feel like a slave with nowhere to turn for relief. Their prison of codependence is worsened because they realize their mistakes in coping with the addicted child have contributed to this grave situation, and the whole thing seems irreversible.

### 18. Total hopelessness and helplessness

These parents now feel there is no way out of the predicament. They overload themselves with remorse, taking full blame for past mistakes with the addicted child.

### 19. Apathy toward problems—and life in general

Exhaustion wins out. They have no more energy to deal with the addicted child. The depression and exhaustion begin to affect employment and all other aspects of life. The parents' apathy is evident in personal grooming and health care. They even may seek medical help for "always feeling tired."

### 20. Increased use of alcohol, drugs, and prescribed medications

These parents' dependence on chemical substances becomes indistinguishable from that of their addicted child. Often this dependence takes a hidden form, such as prescribed medication or compulsive eating. These parents deny any addiction because it *appears* to be different from that of the addicted child; other family members thus accept the falsehood of this appearance and participate in the denial.

## 21. Thoughts of suicide and despair over one's own life

The hopelessness leads to the ultimate despair. Suicide seems imperative because there is "no other way out." Sometimes the codependent parent will attempt suicide.

## 22. Physical and emotional breakdown

The process is completed by a major breakdown in body and mind. Hospitalization may be necessary. Related health problems (such as ulcer and hypertension) are extreme.

# *Reflections*

---

*But the child must grow . . . it must eventually become a completely separate human being. The very essence of motherly love is to care for the child's growth, and that means to want the child's separation from herself.*

—Eric Fromm, The Art of Loving

---

1. Do you find yourself somewhere on the ladder of codependence described above? If so, which stage are you in?

2. Is your spouse on the same ladder? What can you do today to discuss this problem with each other?

# Crazy Like My Child: Marks of the Codependent Parent

---

*My wife played a tape of me arguing with my daughter,
and I couldn't believe it was me talking.
I was out of my head.*

—A codependent father

---

Reuben came to me, suffering from stress. He had seen his family physician because of extreme fatigue, and the doctor ran several tests to determine his condition. All of the tests were negative. Reuben's wife finally convinced him to find a therapist. She had accompanied him when he first came to see me, but Reuben insisted she wait in the outer office while I talked with him.

Reuben began by speaking about his job. He expressed the usual complaints but seemed to have no major irritations at work. I then asked him about home.

**Reuben:** *Oh, it's pretty average. Trudy and I get along all right, I guess. But I wish Elena would find a job—she's my daughter.*

**Farris:** *How old is your daughter?*

**Reuben:** *Uh—twenty-seven. And her daughter is eight years old.*

**Farris:** *How long has Elena been living at home?*

**Reuben:** *About three years, I'd guess. She had to move home because her boyfriend was arrested for drug possession, and she couldn't afford to live alone.*

**Farris:** *Has she had a job?*

**Reuben:** *She does temporary work, on and off.*

**Farris:** *And what does she do with her child when she's gone to work?*

**Reuben:** *We take care of her. Sometimes Elena leaves to visit friends and is gone for a couple of days. We take care of our granddaughter then, too.*

**Farris:** *What do you feel when forced to care for the girl?*

**Reuben:** *I love her very much, but it's difficult not knowing when Elena will be gone, and when she'll return.*

**Farris:** *What do you really think about the whole situation?*

**Reuben** (Beginning to weep): *I feel like I'm going to get sick from it—something fatal, such as cancer or a heart attack. But I don't tell Trudy. She's always praying for Elena, but won't really do anything about the problem. Once I threatened to kick Elena out of the house and keep her girl with us. Trudy was so upset after that fight, she cried the rest of the night. She forced me to promise I'd never threaten our daughter that way again.*

**Farris:** *Reuben, how long do you think you'll be able to tolerate things as they are?*

**Reuben:** *Not much longer, I guess.*

**Farris:** *Will you let me help you—and help your family?*

**Reuben:** *Yes. I hope you can.*

**Farris:** *I believe I can, but I need your wife in the office with us. May I call her in now?*

**Reuben:** *Sure. I certainly hope you can help. We need it.*

I beckoned Trudy into the office and we began to trace their family's history that had led to the present anxieties. Slowly we unraveled the knots of their dilemma.

When codependent parents come to me for help, they typically think they are the only parents in the world with such a problem. On the contrary, they are among thousands of remarkably conspicuous people. I have found that codependent parents usually betray themselves with one of five cries. For the sake of convenience I have labeled these *super-responsible, frazzled, somatic, shamed,* and *powerless.* See if you recognize yourself in any of the following statements.

# The cries of codependent parenting

### The super-responsible parent

*"If I don't take care of things, they just won't get done! Who is going to do them if I don't?"*

The super-responsible parent feels like a victim, albeit a voluntary victim. Such parents have taken upon themselves all of the things other family members have dropped from their lists of responsibilities.

These parents probably were treated badly in childhood and have carried the scars of that experience into parenthood by acting as clean-up person when others "drop the ball." Letting go of burdens for which they are not responsible will require facing the fear that the whole world will crumble if they are not there to take care of everything.

### The frazzled parent

*"I just don't know how much more I can take. I'm at my wits' end!"*

The frazzled parent is exhausted from bearing responsibility when another has been irresponsible and dysfunctional. Such parents may have neglected even their own health to focus on the behavior of another. Often such persons need to rest before facing any other task of changing their lifestyle. However, when attempting to rest, they are usually restless and distracted.

This restlessness occurs because they are not used to just being quiet—and they fear that if they are too quiet, they may have to start facing their own emptiness and meaninglessness because they have neglected to create their own life. Such parents have devoted all attention to others, ignoring their own desires and aspirations.

## The somatic parent

*"I'm so sick myself, and I have to do everything, even though I'm getting worse."*

The somatic parent converts all worry and anxiety into physical symptoms. When a problem rises, somatic parents avoid it with illness rather than addressing it. This tactic is a manipulative device, because illness can be used to produce guilt.

Despite the perceived effectiveness of their behavior, somatic parents are quite unhappy with this situation, because continual sickness is highly unpleasant. After a time this attempt at receiving attention backfires when others, including family members, begin to ignore the parent's perpetual illness.

When faced with the ineffectiveness of their tool of codependence, they feel very lonely. Thus, they are likely to seek change when this manipulation no longer works or when it begins to require too much energy. (Being a somatic parent is emotionally draining.) Hopefully this parent will discover the emotional rewards of reclaiming one's own life.

## The shamed parent

*"It's all my fault. If only I had given her . . . (a better education, more money, et cetera)."*

Shamed parents may have acquired this sense of shame and humiliation earlier in life—possibly as a result of emotional abuse. This sense of inadequacy about their ability to be good parents is a vestige of feelings that arose after disappointing their own parents. Shamed parents may often reproach themselves with "I've failed" or "I haven't given enough."

Regardless of how well or how poorly they have functioned as parents, the matter of the child's behavior remains. Therefore, it is better for such parents to seek a therapist's help to sort out the healthy from the unhealthy in the past; apologize to affected persons for any mistakes; forgive those who have hurt them; and, finally, to continue to address their child's behavior as the separate issue that it really is. Only then can they disentangle the issues of their lives from those of the child's (or with those of the rest of the family). Then the way will be clear for the child to stop focusing on the parents' behavior and begin to acknowledge the destructive behavior in her own life.

## The powerless parent

*"I've tried everything I know to stop her. I can't change a thing."*

In a sense, every codependent parent is a powerless parent—powerless over the actions and attitudes of their child, just as every person is powerless over anyone else's behavior or thoughts. Codependent parents' powerlessness is especially troubling to them, however, because they have, in the past, controlled the child's behavior with threats and rewards. This no longer works.

If the child is an adult, this method of control has lost its effectiveness for a couple of reasons. First, the child may be going through a "break-away" period, which is a normal adolescent experience; drugs and alcohol, however, have simply prolonged this process by retarding emotional growth. Second, the break-away process will continue even after the child enters recovery from drug abuse, because the process is a healthy one. As an adult the child is like all other adults, who must live their own lives by bearing responsibility for their own actions. Powerless parents will learn a difficult lesson through this experience: they can love and advise the child but not control, especially when the child becomes an adult.

Often powerless parents will redirect their thwarted attempts at control toward another family member—another child, a spouse, or even a non-family member—in an effort to restore the control they enjoyed in the past. Any such controlling behavior is yet another attempt to divert attention from their own issues by focusing on the behavior of another.

A self-help group or group therapy will be especially beneficial to such parents. The group will help them confront their powerless parenting with the truth about codependence. They will be forced to answer the question: "Why do I feel a need to control others?"

# Codependent parenting styles

Parents of a dysfunctionally behaving child often adopt a dysfunctional style in dealing with their child. This is because the family develops a system to cope with the problems (with school, finances, and so on) created by the dysfunction. The styles of parental behavior discussed below are typical of the way codependent parents relate to their child's dysfunctional behavior.

You may recognize more than one of these styles in your life. However, one probably will fit best, because you began the pattern early in your child's life (when she started using drugs and acting irresponsibly) by reacting to her behavior in a specific way.

Recognizing your pattern of reaction is the first major step toward change. Once aware of your own actions you will have greater ability to choose the response you desire and to work toward changing yourself. This will be the key to changing the unhealthy family system that has enabled your child's irresponsible behavior.

## The rescuer

No matter what the child's age, if she is in financial, legal, or physical (for example, intoxicated) trouble, rescuer parents will offer time, money, a car, a house, et cetera, to deliver the child again. Such parents willingly neglect their own needs to take care of the needs of their child.

## The enabler

Wanting desperately to be needed, enabler parents will work stalwartly to ensure that the adult child continues her use of chemical substances or addictive behavior. Enablers accomplish this by sabotaging the child's attempts to change and by making excuses for that child's failure to seek treatment, continue sobriety, and maintain a healthy lifestyle.

Enablers need to take care of their adult child. Their sense of being needed is sustained by the dysfunction and dependence of their adult child. They will unconsciously sabotage treatment because it threatens their ability to be needed.

## The scapegoat

Mea culpa (through my fault) is the life motto of every scapegoat parent. These parents not only blame themselves for the problems caused by their child's dysfunctional behavior, but they allow the child (and sometimes the rest of the family) to blame these problems on them. The parent, then, is seen as "the real problem." Assuming a role they probably learned in childhood and have carried into adulthood, scapegoats are accustomed to being "the problem" and thus fit easily into a victim role.

## The forgotten parent

Partly because of embarrassment over their child's situation and partly because their life now revolves totally around the child, forgotten parents withdraw from interaction with friends and other family members and avoid most social situations. The parents' hearts are broken because they no longer are special to the child. Such parents crave attention from the child (probably because of a lack of attention in their own early life) and lavish the child with attention, expecting to receive it in return.

Parents with such expectations will fail to attain undivided love because the child, overwhelmed by such a demand, rebels against it (such as with drug use). Forgotten parents therefore must slowly learn to live their own lives, rather than depending on the child for gratification. If they learn this their interactions with the child will be healthy, marked by mutual giving rather than being filled with need.

## The silent partner

Keeping the problem at arm's length, the silent partner parent allows his partner to shoulder the responsibility of dealing with the dysfunctional behavior of the child—thus forcing the partner to embrace one of the other codependent parenting styles. Silent partners say nothing and do nothing in the relationship with the child. Not surprisingly, they may display a similar uninvolved style in the spousal relationship. (Caution: the silent partner parents may be trying to conceal their own addiction.)

## The mascot

"She's just having fun" or "He's just sowing his wild oats" are common excuses given by mascot parents for their child's dysfunctional behavior. In an attempt to laugh along and be a "pal" to the child, they treat lightly the addiction and other dysfunctions. They may even drink or use drugs with the child, thus creating or worsening their own addiction problem.

Fearing the world of adulthood, with its responsibilities and decisions, these parents become fixated in adolescent behavior rather than facing the reality of their own aging. Their self-esteem is based on immature notions. They need, through therapy, to return to adolescence and work out the causes of obsession with being a "buddy" to others who actually are adolescents.

## The dependent parent

"I can handle my liquor, but I'm worried about my daughter," says the dependent parent. By focusing on the problems of their adult child, dependent parents think they can hide their own chemical addiction problems. This is denial in its purest form.

Such parents need to be confronted by other family members about their own addiction before helping to confront the child about her addiction and dysfunctional behavior. Because this is a separate case of addiction, such parents cannot afford the luxury of discussing the chemical dependence of any other family member. All of their attention and energy need to focus on their own path of recovery. Hopefully such parents will choose the proper treatment for their addiction.

## The professional codependent

Here is a parent who has heard all of the codependence jargon at countless meetings and workshops on the subject. They know the concepts and therapeutic language by heart. They roam from one self-help group meeting to another, reciting the plight of their child's dysfunctional life and giving the impression of being a martyr to any who will listen to this tale of woe.

Contrary to their doleful stories, professional codependent parents are never serious about examining their own codependence and its resultant behavior. Neither will they accept any suggestions from others that might change the unhealthy relationship with the addicted child. These parents fear ending the codependence because this relationship affords the central meaning for life and a focus that seems easier than confronting their own unhealthy behavior and attitudes.

## The Jekyll-Hyde parent

Inconsistency marks the behavior of such parents, whose reactions to the irresponsibility of their child flip-flop from one extreme to the other. Initially angry and determined, these parents usually blast their child, threatening expulsion from the house, curtailment of funds, and so on. Within a few days, however, they are engulfed by feelings of inadequacy and guilt over their performance as a parent. They therefore repent of their punitive measures.

Inconsistent in responding to the child's dysfunctional behavior, they are easily manipulated by the child's threats and tears and usually give the child another chance. They believe that, somehow, things will magically be different this time.

# *Reflections*

1. Write down two or three of the statements you use most frequently when speaking about your child.

2. What are the usual things said by your spouse when discussing your child?

3. Which of the above cries and styles most closely resemble your own? In what situations do they most frequently surface?

# *Crazy, but Organized: The Rules of Codependent Parenting*

*Today I have got out of all trouble, or rather I have cast out all trouble, for it was not outside, but within, in my opinions.*

—Marcus Aurelius, Meditations

While teaching a workshop in 1991 on codependence and parents, I decided to produce a tongue-in-cheek set of rules for how one should conduct the process of being a codependent parent. I was surprised at how well my audience responded to the list and at how effective it was in helping people recognize their codependence. Here it is:

## Rules of Codependent Parenting

1. My problems as a parent are not as important as the problems of my child.

2. I don't express my negative feelings because they might upset my child (who might therefore leave me).

3. I must communicate with my child through a family messenger (especially if the message is a criticism).

4.   Focusing on my needs as an individual is selfish and there-fore must be avoided

5.   I must be the perfect parent, even though I have to hide my inadequacies.

6.   I must avoid facing my own addictions by focusing time and energy on the problems of my child.

7.   I must avoid facing the problems of my marriage (or my love relationships, if I am not married) by focusing time and energy on my child.

8.   I must remember that the world is very serious, so I must not allow time to enjoy myself (especially if my child could get into trouble while I am relaxing).

9.   I must not rock the family boat by alienating my child with any mention of limits on her behavior.

10.  I will always feel responsible for my child's actions and, after covering up for the harmful actions, I must always give my child another chance under the same conditions as before (i.e., I believe everything will magically improve without my changing the situation).

# Understanding the rules of codependent parenting

Here are examples from family situations that illustrate how these rules of codependence work. Do any of these seem familiar to you?

## 1. My problems as a parent are not as important as the problems of my child

Eugenia was running low on cash. This was not because her retirement income was inadequate. She had saved during her career through a pension fund at work and through stock purchases she and her late husband had made. In addition, her housing expenses were low.

Unfortunately, Eugenia was increasingly have trouble making ends meet because Phil, her son, was always borrowing money (and rarely repaying her). She needed this month's dividend money to have her teeth treated by the dentist. However, she would forego the visit because Phil needed the money for his car.

She sometimes asked herself how his car could break down so often, but she avoided the answer. Though suspicious that he used the money for drugs, she never would mention this to Phil or anyone else. Anyway, Phil was young, and she had lived her life. He deserved a chance to do well—and between drugs and three difficult marriages he had already endured so many problems. His problems were much larger than hers.

## 2. I don't express my negative feelings because they might upset my child (who might therefore leave me)

Eugenia also feared mentioning to Phil his behavior at the Fourth of July barbecue. During the affair he had upset the entire family by getting drunk and throwing the barbecue grill into the swimming pool. He then had driven away in his car. Luckily, he didn't crash.

Eugenia refused to intervene. And when Phil's brother Jerry wanted to call the police to stop him, Eugenia threatened to never again speak to Jerry if he did so. (How could he dare turn in his own brother to the police!) Jerry subsequently left the party in anger also.

Four months later the family was planning to eat Thanksgiving dinner together. Eugenia was hoping that if everyone would just forget about the July incident, the Thanksgiving celebration would go smoothly. She avoided discussion of the Fourth of July with Phil because she feared he would get angry at her raising the issue and thus skip the Thanksgiving dinner. After all, Phil, all alone now after his third divorce, needed the company. Eugenia hoped that the other family members would understand and keep silent about his earlier behavior.

## 3. I must communicate with my child through a family messenger (especially if the message is a criticism)

Only with great difficulty had Dan ever expressed his emotions to any of his children. Now that his wife had died and was no longer present to talk with the children about their problems, Dan had been using his daughter Nancy to assume that duty.

Unfortunately, this means of communication didn't seem to be working for his son Hal.

Hal was living at Dan's home since getting out of jail for driving under the influence of alcohol. Dan reasoned, of course, that this arrangement would help Hal to save money so that he could be on his own again. However, Hal was spending no money on groceries and was disturbing his father's sleep by staying up late. In addition, Hal's girlfriend was spending the night at the house once or twice each week.

Weary and frustrated, Dan decided to ask Nancy to confront Hal about the arrangement. After all, she had always talked to Hal in the past when Dan had a problem with him. "She seems like a substitute mother for Hal," thought Dan, "and maybe that's what he needs right now."

## 4. Focusing on my needs as an individual is selfish and therefore must be avoided

Things were getting worse for Dan. His home had become a nightly drinking haven for Hal and his cronies, and now Hal's girlfriend was living in the house. No longer feeling comfortable in his own house, Dan often would leave during the evening to get away from Hal and his friends.

Dan wanted to speak to Hal about the whole matter, but the last time he had started to do so, Hal pointed out that Dan had paid for his daughter Nancy's education yet didn't even care about supporting his son for just a few months. Hal accused his father of making money more important than his own children and of saving for his own retirement without any concern for Hal's present problems. Feeling guilty, Dan backed down, but he felt more helpless and miserable than ever.

## 5. I must be the perfect parent, even though I have to hide my own inadequacies

Joanne talked to no one about the problems she and her husband were having with Gary, their son. His drug use was bad enough, but now he had been arrested and jailed. Extremely embarrassed, she avoided seeing any of her friends, afraid they might know about Gary's problems.

Neither did Joanne ever mention any of Gary's misdeeds to her siblings in Ohio—they all seemed to have "perfect" families.

Each of their children had attended college and had a good job. No one in her family ever mentioned problems with drugs or the police. Her mother was extremely proud that all of her children had married and none had divorced. With such family pressure, Joanne felt she could never admit Gary's mistakes.

## 6. I must avoid facing my own addictions by focusing time and energy on the problems of my child

Joanne felt continually upset about Gary's behavior; she was even having difficulty getting enough rest and being able to relax. The doctor had prescribed her some tranquilizers, and some days she thought she would not survive without the pills. She kept them with her throughout the day.

Not wanting to become addicted, Joanne took only a small bit of a pill when she needed it. Although this method sometimes seemed to use up the pills faster, she assured herself, "I think it's okay. The doctor said they're not addictive. And besides, I need them. How can I help Gary if I'm so nervous myself?"

## 7. I must avoid facing the problems of my marriage (or my love relationships, if I am not married) by focusing time and energy on my child

Joanne was infuriated by Morris, her husband. Believing their son, Gary, would stop using drugs if he only had more communication with his father, Joanne had begged Morris to spend more time talking to Gary. To her dismay, Morris seemed uninterested in their son.

In fact, Morris seemed angry at everyone, often snapping at Joanne or just ignoring her. He used to be tender and attentive. Now he seemed almost invisible—most days he worked late and sometimes he stayed out with friends. His sexual relationship with Joanne was almost nonexistent. Joanne recalled how they used to be so close, but now their personalities seemed completely different.

Joanne felt abandoned. Her dreams about marriage seemed shattered. If Morris would only spend time with her to help Gary, it would all change and then she could be attentive to him again. But right now, Gary needed her most.

## 8. I must remember that the world is very serious, so I must not allow time to enjoy myself (especially if my child could get into trouble while I am relaxing)

Joanne and Morris had been planning a dream vacation to Europe. In order to save money for the trip they even had forgone buying a new car. They wanted the vacation so badly, and the old car could last another year.

But now they didn't want to risk leaving Gary for three weeks. He could get into serious trouble if they didn't watch over him. And if he did get into trouble, they wouldn't be around to help him. Besides, Gary needed the money they would have spent on the vacation. He said he needed money for a car so that he could find a job. He had lost his last three jobs because his employers were so unfair, and now he was having such a terrible time finding another.

"It's a good thing we're around, or Gary would be out on the streets," said Joanne. Morris said nothing.

## 9. I must not rock the family boat by alienating my child with any mention of limits on her behavior

Neil had never been so angry. His daughter Marian, just fired for her numerous absences, could no longer keep her part of the agreement that she would pay rent for living with her parents. And they had made the agreement only one week before!

Despite his frustration, Neil insisted that he couldn't throw Marian out of the house. Phyllis, his wife, would hit the ceiling. "Where would a young girl go?" she had argued the last time the two had discussed the matter.

Now Neil hated being at home, and he didn't know what to do about it. His daughter seemed to do whatever she wanted, and when her parents challenged her behavior, she would cry and threaten to kill herself. He said he felt as if he were living in hell, trapped on a lower level. Sometimes he wished he, instead of Marian, were the one taking the drugs.

## 10. I will always feel responsible for my child's actions and, after covering up for the harmful actions, I must always give my child another chance under the same conditions as before (i.e., I believe everything will magically improve without my changing the situation)

When Marian called to announce she had been in a car accident, Phyllis feared someone had died. She also feared Marian would go to jail, because she was on probation after her last arrest for driving under the influence of alcohol. Fortunately, no one was injured, and Morris had been able to convince the other driver not to call the police or the insurance companies. Morris would pay for any repairs.

He estimated that the bill would be about $2,000, but that seemed a small price for keeping Marian out of jail—during her last stay in jail she was hysterical, and Phyllis had been the same. Maybe, after this near miss with the law, Marian would see the severity of her problem. This would be a good lesson for her, realizing that she could have gone to jail again.

"This will scare Marian for a while," thought Phyllis, "and maybe she'll finally let us help her."

> *The person who won't grow up, who remains irresponsible, addicted, and dependent, usually has a codependent enabling him to remain immature. A codependent always needs to be needed. This is a codependent's reason for living.*

# *Reflections*

1.   What was the most recent incident in your family that revealed codependent behavior?

2.   As you recall the event, what are your opinions about it? What are your feelings about it?

# Love versus Codependence

---

*Love is letting go of fear.*

—Gerald Jampolsky

---

How can I know the difference between healthy love and codependence when I'm dealing with my child? It is a question I hear often. Confronted with the idea that they may be codependent, parents typically find themselves confused about the difference.

My usual answer comes as a question: "Are you in a mutual relationship with your child? Does he care as much about your welfare as you care about his?"

A parent naturally cares more about the child than the child cares about the parent. But when that child exhibits almost no concern (unless they will benefit by that concern—for example, Mom will give me money if I stop in for Christmas dinner) while the parent is extremely concerned about him, there exists an imbalance. Such disparity in the relationship tells me the parent is acting as a codependent.

# The marks of love and codependence

The comparison table below will help parents analyze their behavior toward their child. Although this should not be used as the final analysis for diagnosing codependency, it can be very helpful in raising one's awareness of the difference between codependent and healthy, loving behavior.

## Love

## Codependence

| Love | Codependence |
| --- | --- |
| I will make sure my child grows up knowing that he must learn from (and pay the consequences of) mistakes and poor choices. | I will protect my child from all negative consequences and cover up for his mistakes. |
| I and my child have separate lives. I am focused on my life and my child is focused on his. | My child's life is the focus of my life. I will live my life for my child, no matter how old he may be. |
| I am responsible for my life, and my child is responsible for his. I can help, but I will not take responsibility for his actions. | I am responsible for my child's actions because they reflect on the quality of my parenting. I will try to cover up for his mistakes to save myself embarrassment. |
| I trust my child and accept the risks of that trust—if he makes mistakes, that is his business. I don't need to constantly wonder about and pry into his activities. | I cannot trust my child because my past trust has been violated. I therefore will pry into his life constantly to find out if he is meeting my expectations for his life. I will maneuver my child away from anything I consider inappropriate or harmful. |
| I can look at my own life and evaluate it rather than avoiding self-analysis. I can be honest with myself about myself. | I must avoid looking at my own life because I fear discovering faults that are hard to admit. I will, instead, focus on the life of my child. |

Life is sometimes difficult, and my child must learn that this is so. If I protect my child from the difficulties of life, I will impede his maturing into a responsible adult.

Life is sometimes difficult, but my child must be shielded from this fact. I must, therefore, at any cost to my family or me, protect my child so he need not face the consequences of his actions or develop a sense of responsibility for his life choices.

# A story of letting go

*And [Jesus] said, "There was a man who had two sons; and the younger of them said to his father, 'Father, give me the share of property that falls to me.' And he divided his living between them. Not many days later, the younger son gathered all he had and took his journey into a far country, and there he squandered all his property in loose living. And when he had spent everything, a great famine arose in that country, and he began to be in want. So he went and joined himself to one of the citizens of that country who sent him into his fields to feed swine. And he would gladly have fed on the pods that the swine ate; and no one gave him anything. But when he came to himself he said, 'How many of my father's hired servants have bread enough and to spare, but I perish here with hunger! I will arise and go to my father, and I will say to him, 'Father, I have sinned against heaven and before you; I am no longer worthy to be called your son; treat me as one of your hired servants.' And he arose and came to his father. But while he was yet at a distance, his father saw him and had compassion, and ran and embraced him and kissed him. And the son said to him, 'Father, I have sinned against heaven and before you; I am no longer worthy to be called your son.' But the father said to his servants, 'Bring quickly the best robe, and put it on him; and put a ring on his hand, and shoes on his feet; and bring the fatted calf and kill it, and let us eat and make merry; for this my son was dead, and is alive again; he was lost, and is found.'"*

—Luke 15:11-24

The parable of the prodigal son is a perfect story for codependent parents. It is a story that shows a father allowing his son, a young man, to choose the wrong path. Given the right to choose, while no doubt disregarding the advice of his father and other adults, he disappeared with his inheritance and squandered it in what I interpret to have been dysfunctional behavior—likely alcohol abuse as well as other deviant behaviors.

Although knowing he could not change his son, the father still deeply loved his wayward son. The fact that he saw the son returning at a distance implies he had been looking each day for him, longing for his return. He even may have had a premonition of his son's return (as parents often do). All of this points to the father's love.

The striking element of this story is that the father *let go* of his son. He did not act codependently, arguing with him and fighting. Nor did he plead with the young man to stay. He let go of the young man, aware of the future his son probably had chosen. Then he waited for the day when his son would—as is often the case with an alcoholic—"hit bottom" (or as the story says, "he came to himself").

We learn a profound truth from the example in this parable: *the true meaning of love is letting go.* The father let go of the son but never once let go of his love for him. When his son came to his senses, the father was waiting, still ready to love and forgive, ready to welcome him into his house. Nonetheless, the father did not budge one inch; his son had to change, had to leave behind a life of addiction that had sunk him to a sorry state after spending everything on alcohol and drinking companions. The father stood firm on his principles and on his love for his son. It was not easy. But we recognize his choice was healthy and wise.

# *Reflections*

*The truth is always the strongest argument.*

—Sophocles

1. What are your reactions to this parable after reading it in the light of your understanding of codependence?

2. How has this understanding helped you to make any decisions about the way you will deal with your child in the future?

## PART TWO

# Recovering from Parental Codependence

# *What Is Love?*

---

*Love does not insist on its own way; it is not irritable or resentful; it does not rejoice at wrong, but rejoices in the right.*

—1 Corinthians 13:5, 6

---

A couple came to my office asking for help with their thirty-year-old son. In and out of hospitals for treatment of his drug abuse, he had caused his parents great emotional damage and had also cost them about $35,000 in auto repairs, legal fees, and medical bills. This son was now asking for another car, having destroyed his last one in yet another accident.

My advice was simple. "Let go of your son. Refuse to pay any more of his expenses. Don't allow him to live at home until he gains a job, and until he stops sneaking drugs into the house."

They were horrified. The mother began to cry and the father said to me, "We can't do that! You know we're Christians, that we're taught to love one another. We love each of our children, and we can't turn our backs on this son. Can't you help us with this situation?"

"I will help you," I replied, then opened the Bible to the Gospel of John (4:16-19):

Jesus said to [the woman at the well], "Go, call your husband, and come here." The woman answered him, "I have no husband." Jesus said to her, "You are right in saying, 'I have no husband'; for you have had five husbands, and he whom you now have is not your husband; this you said truly." The woman said to him, Sir, I perceive that you are a prophet."

"Do you see," I asked the couple, "that Jesus had love for this woman?" They nodded. "Do you also see," I continued, "that Jesus had to act upon that love by telling her the truth—that he had to confront her with the fact that she had been married five times and had still not found the happiness she was seeking? That she was still unfulfilled and unhappy?" They sat in silence.

Finally I challenged, "Will you do with your son the same thing Jesus did with this woman? Will you tell the truth—that he is addicted and miserable, and that you'll no longer participate in this unhappy situation?" They shifted awkwardly in their chairs. "If you want to help your son, tell him the truth—and admit the truth to yourselves."

Although fearful of the consequences, they agreed to change. They discovered the courage to go home and to act on my suggestions to stop participating in their son's addiction, to stop supporting him with a home, money, and a car.

Teachers of the Bible sometimes point to a passage and state, "This was Jesus's first healing," or "This was Jesus's first miracle." I like to point to the story of the woman at the well and declare, "This was Jesus's first 'intervention.'" As with the story of the prodigal son, I find it a forceful tool in helping parents recognize their codependence.

## Ten keys to loving an addicted person

The New Testament story I used above inspired me to outline ten principles that can guide parents in truly loving an addicted child. As those Christian parents who thought they must act codependently to fulfill Jesus's standard of family love, many parents confuse love with rescuing and enabling behaviors.

Following are ten guidelines for true love—love that is measured by truth and tempered by compassion. I trust these principles will help you in the difficult task of discriminating between love (which may be painful) and codependence (which is more painful in the long run).

## 1. Stop denying the reality of drug abuse and irresponsibility

Denial is the lie of codependence. It is the "elephant in the living room" that the family tries to ignore. Face the fact that a family member is addicted. This is the first step in restoring the family to health.

## 2. Affirm the reality of drug abuse and irresponsibility

When talking to the addicted person, don't merely talk in generalities, but give real instances of irresponsibility and specific examples of drug abuse behavior. Specific evidence makes it more difficult to deny this type of behavior or to get sidetracked on issues that are unrelated to drug and alcohol use.

## 3. Admit your own failures without excusing the addicted person's prolonged irresponsibility

Admitting your own mistakes is difficult. If you admit them, however, you can forsake those mistakes and start to focus again on the real issue: your child's drug abuse.

## 4. Offer the addicted person alternatives to the drug abuse and irresponsible behavior, but do not choose the alternative

The addicted person must make the choice and thus begin taking responsibility for the consequences of her choices. A healthy choice means healthy consequences and an unhealthy choice means continued disaster. You can help by responding to her honest questions about these choices, not by making the choice.

## 5. Do not argue if that person chooses an alternative different from the one you would have chosen

The addicted person may be unaware of the number of options she has to choose from. Even if the addict makes the wrong choice, usually the mistake can be corrected and she can learn from the error.

If you think the choice is life threatening, ask someone else for advice before choosing to further involve yourself in the decision. (An example of this might be preventing the addicted person from driving under the influence of alcohol or drugs. You cannot change the addict's decision to drive under such circumstances, but you may, for example, choose to call the police.)

Remember that for the addicted person, merely to take responsibility for a choice is, in itself, a good choice. It is the beginning of responsible behavior and recovery.

## 6. Don't argue if the person chooses to return to drug abuse

Don't allow the addicted person to return responsibility to you. The addict's choice to abuse drugs and alcohol is not your responsibility. You do not, however, have to tolerate the addicted person's living rent-free, borrowing your money, and so on.

## 7. Keep the door open for the day that person will finally leave drug abuse and the irresponsibility that accompanies that lifestyle

You can never tell what the future holds. The situations that seem hopeless can surprise you and change. Do not doom yourself to the same sense of hopelessness as the person who is addicted. Otherwise you will trap yourself in codependent anger.

## 8. Do not transfer your codependence to another person

Avoid the temptation to take care of someone else in order to take the focus off your own recovery from codependence. Give yourself a break. Focus on your own life so you can improve it. You deserve the love from yourself that will allow you to take care of yourself.

## 9. Work on your own program of recovery from codependence

Don't live in denial of your own unhealthy lifestyle. Therapy and a self-help group will reinforce the recovery process, acting as mirrors for your behavior. Through the eyes of others familiar with your experience, you will see yourself in a new way and change the behavior that has contributed to your frustration and general unhappiness.

## 10. Check your own life for addictive behavior

Do not deny the addictions in your own life. These may be addictions to drugs, alcohol, prescribed medication, food, tobacco, gambling, or sex. Any behavior that seems to control your life and adds to your unhappiness may be an addiction.

Take the same advice you are giving to your addicted child by seeking recovery. Find help for your behavior through a group or counselor with experience in helping addicted people. Take courage, you can change and be happy and healthy.

Time and patience are the keys to your relationship with your child. In time, and with patient endurance, you will find serenity and, hopefully, your child will find sobriety and serenity. It is my hope that you find serenity soon and that it becomes a treasure you share with your entire family.

# *Reflections*

---

*Time is . . .*
*Too slow for those who wait,*
*Too swift for those who fear,*
*Too long for those who grieve,*
*Too short for those who rejoice;*
*But for those who love,*
*Time is eternity.*
—Henry Van Dyke

*Time ripens all things. No man is born wise.*

—Cervantes

---

1.  Do you have a secret agenda for your child? Do you feel successful only if your child fulfills your agenda (finishes school, gives up drugs, gets married, and so forth, according to your timetable)? How do you feel when your expectations are not met?

2.  How are you taking time for yourself? In what ways have you enjoyed your life in the past week? How have you improved your own life, apart from the life of your child?

# A Sample Intervention: The Story of Blair and Her Family

---

*Know thyself.*

—Socrates

---

The following story of Blair and her family traces the events from the time her parents first sought help, to Blair's treatment and recovery process. It provides a good example of parents who learned how to aid to their daughter effectively, how to love without feeling guilty, controlling, or helpless.

At her parents' first visit to my office, Blair was twenty-two years old. She was the only child born out of Ted and Irma's present marriage, though Irma had two children and Ted had one from previous marriages. When they first came to the office, Irma was angry and talkative, while Ted sat very quietly, barely participating in the conversation.

## Full circle

**Farris:** *Would you tell me about your life with Blair?*

**Irma:** *It's very difficult. Blair is not living at home now because we had a fight with her—she had come home after a three-day binge with her friends. They drink and use drugs, and just go off into their little drug world. She was such a good girl when she was young. She used to be pretty, but now she looks like a burned-out hooker. Anyway, I got mad at her and we had a big fight. We always get into these fights.*

**Farris:** *Ted, what did you say to Blair at this time?*

**Ted:** *Not much. Irma talks to her better than I do.*

**Irma:** *Yes, and that's part of the problem. Ted doesn't help me with the family. He wants to leave when I talk to Blair, or he just stays out of the conversation. He's Mr. Silent. What can I do to get this man to help me get our daughter off of drugs?*

**Farris:** *May I ask about your attempts to help Blair in the past?*

**Irma:** *We tried four years ago to help by taking her to a counselor. That didn't work. She went for a while and even stopped using drugs for two or three months. Then she returned to the drugs and to drinking. She goes to parties where all her friends whoop it up with booze and drugs.*

*We also tried to help her two years ago by sending her to live with my sister in Oregon, but she just caused trouble there. She's been in and out of the house—because when we fight, she leaves. Now she's living with her sister, my daughter, in an apartment near our home.*

**Farris:** *Now let me ask about your own lives before we continue to talk about Blair. Will you tell me about your relationship? Do you think it is strong?*

**Irma:** *Oh, we fight—but we get along most of the time.*

**Farris:** *Ted, do you want to add your viewpoint?*

**Ted:** *Oh, Irma's right. We fight, but we generally get along.*

**Farris:** *How about alcohol or drugs? How often do you use them?*

**Irma:** *Drugs? We don't use drugs! We're trying to get Blair off drugs. We don't use them.*

**Farris:** *Alcohol? How do you use alcohol?*

**Irma:** *Oh, Ted might have a couple of beers at night.*

We would later discover that Ted had a severe alcohol problem (see chapter 10).

**Farris:** *Let's go back to Blair. Do you think we could have a meeting with family members—and other people important in Blair's life? I'd like to have as many together as possible to plan for confronting Blair about her drug use. I'm available next Tuesday evening.*

**Irma:** *I think we could do that. Where do you want us to meet?*

**Farris:** *How about at your home? Will you arrange that? You need to invite as many as possible who are connected with Blair—except her crowd of drug friends.*

**Irma:** *Yes, I can arrange that. What will I tell them?*

**Farris:** *Tell them we're meeting to find a way to help Blair before she kills herself, and that I'll be there.*

**Irma:** *I'll make the phone calls.*

# Intervention

Intervention is the presentation of the *facts* of dysfunctional behavior to a member of the family or a friend who is addicted to drugs or alcohol. Though conducted by family members or involved friends, the event should be performed under the guidance of a professional counselor acquainted with intervention methods.

An intervention begins with one or more preparation sessions in which the participants meet to air their concerns about the addicted family member. In such a session they will discuss memories of specific instances in which they saw the addicted person under the influence of alcohol or drugs; they will describe the effects of the addiction and their feelings about those incidents. They will then write down the things they have discussed during these sessions to save for the intervention session.

The actual intervention session brings together the addicted person and the concerned people so they can present their written material and speak in general to the addicted family member.

The purpose is to present the evidence of the dysfunctional behavior.

The element of surprise is important at an intervention, to ensure that the individual does not avoid the meeting. This sudden jolt of reality will, hopefully, break through the addict's denial as family members and friends from school, work, and elsewhere declare, "We are aware of your addiction—and it is wrecking your life as well as affecting our lives." Confronted so powerfully with the reality of her addiction, the person usually consents to treatment. With the help and preparation of the professional counselor, the addicted family member will immediately enter a treatment program.

Obviously, intervention is helpful to the addicted person. Less obvious is the positive effect intervention has on the family members and friends who participate. They, too, begin a process of dealing with their denial. For too long they have not dealt effectively with the addicted person. At the intervention session, however, they are able to honestly assess their feelings and reactions to past negative experiences. This healing experience injects a sense of hope and adequacy to deal with the problem of addiction. This, of course, is not the end of the story. However, it is a fresh start for both the addicted family member and for those who are affected by that person's addiction.

## Preparing for Blair's intervention

Blair's intervention began with a planning meeting held by her family members. As they sat together and told their stories about being with Blair, they recalled specific times when Blair was drugged, drunk, or both. Some cried as they talked about the loss they felt watching their baby sister, the once pretty little girl, living as a drug addict.

Each person was asked to write a short letter to Blair and bring it to the intervention (at a brother's home, where she occasionally came for dinner). Each letter was to contain two parts. One part would address a specific incident in which Blair was under the influence of alcohol or drugs and describe how she acted irresponsibly when she used the substances. The second part would tell how much the writer cared about Blair and her health and happiness. We would meet in one week.

Happily, almost everyone was writing a letter to Blair, and as the week passed, some family members even called to ask advice on their letters. Meanwhile, I called a local drug and alcohol treatment clinic to arrange Blair's immediate enrollment in the program—if she chose to cooperate with the intervention. (If the intervention is carefully planned, the person will consent to immediately entering the treatment program. We were prepared to have Blair do just that.)

When the evening of the intervention arrived, everyone was ready. Blair had agreed to come for dinner with her family but knew nothing of the intervention. As she entered and saw everyone sitting in a large circle, she realized that something different was about to happen and that it involved her.

## Blair's moment of truth

**Blair:** *What are you all doing? Why are you sitting around like this—and who is he* (pointing toward me)*?*

**Irma:** *That's Dr. Farris, Blair, and—*

**Farris:** *Blair, if I may interrupt your mother for a moment, I want to tell you what we are doing here.*

**Blair:** *You don't have to tell me. I know you're here to talk to me. Well, I'm not staying!*

**Farris:** *Blair, you may choose to leave, but I want to ask you just one small favor. Your sister has something to read to you. Would you listen to her for just five minutes? After that you can leave. Would you do that?*

**Blair:** *Okay, but I want to stand by the door.*

**Farris:** *Stand or sit anywhere, but just listen for five minutes. No one will stop you from leaving after that—if you choose to do so. Your sister Charlene wants to read something to you. You live with her. Would you just listen to her?* (I turn to the sister.) *Charlene, start reading.*

Charlene began to read—and almost immediately began to cry as well. Her letter to Blair was filled with stories of Blair's being drunk or on drugs, coming home late.

Charlene recounted her fear when Blair, under the influence of drugs, drove around with Charlene's little daughter and son. She told of the deep hurt she felt when Blair would argue heatedly after coming home in the middle of the night from partying with her drug friends. She read about the destruction caused when Blair fell against the stereo equipment after drinking all night. Then she confessed how much she loved Blair and how heartbroken she felt over the loss of their relationship because of Blair's use of drugs and alcohol.

Blair began to cry. Most of the family members cried also as they took turns reading their letters to Blair. Blair was soon slumped on the floor, sobbing as she vented a flood of emotions trapped by her use of emotion-dulling drugs. By the end of the evening she was ready to enter a treatment program; Charlene, Irma, and Ted immediately took her to the center where I had made arrangements.

This was the beginning of the road to recovery, the beginning of positive upheaval in the lives of both Blair and her family members. More than they could ever guess, Blair's transformation would alter their own lives. Their roles as codependents would change as Blair became healthier by her recovery. In addition, this recovery would allow the parents, brothers and sisters, and friends to focus on their own foibles and thus become honest about changes needed in their own lives.

# *Reflections*

1. What would be your greatest fear in participating in an intervention for someone you love?

2. What would you write to your child about her behavior and her use of drugs or alcohol?

# After the Intervention: Surviving the Atomic Blast

> *Although I was confronting my daughter about her drugs, I couldn't stop thinking about myself and all my drinking. I was an alcoholic—and I felt like a hypocrite. It was then that I decided to get some help.*
>
> —Ted, a recovering alcoholic

## Fallout

Although it may seem bizarre, it happens almost every time. As one family member begins to gain health through recovery from drug and alcohol abuse, new problems arise, often because another person takes the position of being "the problem."

One week after Blair entered the treatment unit, her father embarked on a rip-roaring, drunken binge that lasted five days. This, it became apparent, was not new behavior for Ted. He had been drinking all along, but both Ted and Irma had chosen not to reveal this fact to me when they came for help.

Ted had always contended he could handle his use of alcohol. And Irma, although not believing him, felt that finding help for Blair was more important. She had, after all, lived with Ted's alcoholism for twenty-three years. And although it had worsened over the years, she had created a way to cope with it, often using it to threaten Ted when he hindered her plans for their lives.

Some of the family members came together to perform an intervention for Ted, and soon he entered a hospital treatment program as well. During Ted's treatment Irma, now alone, began participating in individual and group sessions to address her own codependence.

The group sessions showed Irma that her behavior had exhausted her. She had created a family position for herself in which she clenched the control and the responsibility for many members of her family—especially for Ted and Blair. Irma struggled acutely as she discovered more and more of her rescuing and enabling behavior.

As she became aware of the control she had exercised over Ted's and Blair's lives, she also talked about her fears and sadness at the loss of hope and joy in her marriage and in her love for her children. She also admitted her extreme fatigue. And during other therapy sessions Irma talked about her childhood and her mother's drinking. While this was painful, it lifted Irma out of the deep pit of helplessness called codependence.

Ted went through a similar ordeal of looking back through his life to confront his own alcoholism. This was all part of the treatment program initiated in the hospital, and it continued in a residential treatment center—a special program for treating chemical dependence.

Ted began facing his guilt and hopelessness. He also began to talk more, to express his own thoughts and feelings that had been bottled up for years. Now they seemed to pour out of his mind and heart. He also began taking initiative in family issues; realizing he and Irma had much to deal with once he was finished with the treatment center, he began holding family sessions with her.

# Family contracts after treatment

After the addicted person has completed a treatment program the family may want to create a contract with him. Such a contract sets limits on the participation of family members in enabling the addiction process and in any future relapse experience. In other words, a contract is a way to follow through after the intervention.

In a contract codependent family members declare they will no longer continue specific behaviors that helped perpetuate the addicted person's behavior. The contract may set limits on how much money a codependent parent may spend on the addicted family member as well as how long the recovering person may stay in the family home, should she relapse.

When Blair completed her residential treatment program her family composed a contract like this:

Dear Blair,

We, your parents, and I, your sister, Charlene, wish you the best because we love you. We are happy that you finally sought help in dealing with your drug addiction, and we hope you continue on the road to recovery.

As you have been recovering, we have been facing our own behavior in our relationships with you. As a result, we have decided to make some changes as well. These are the changes we need to make:

First of all, we will no longer loan or give you money, other than the money set aside by your parents for your twenty-fourth birthday, just as your brothers and sisters received on their twenty-fourth birthdays. Normal gifts of money for birthdays, etc. will still be a matter of personal choice.

We will not, however, give you any special gifts, and we will not—for one year—provide any aid in buying a car, condominium, or other major item. We hope that during this year you will continue your recovery program. This will be important, not only for our relationship, but also for future decisions about money in our relationship.

Second, you may choose to live in either of our homes, but only temporarily. We expect you to plan to live on your own after one year. By saving money, and by staying clean and sober, we hope you will be ready for this responsibility. If, however, you begin to use drugs again, you will not be welcome in either of our homes and thus will be asked to leave.

Third, you may not bring any drugs or drug-using

friends into our homes. If you do either of these, we will ask you to leave immediately.

Fourth, in whichever home you live, you will participate in keeping the home clean and will have dinner at home three nights a week. This will allow us to live in a family relationship, yet allow you freedom to pursue your own life and other relationships.

Please understand how much we love you and want you able to take care of yourself, because we now realize the need to care for ourselves rather than be codependent with you. Should you decide not to live with us, we are prepared to accept your decision, for we want to be a family; we want to have healthy love for each other and spend time together, no matter where you choose to live. And we want you and each of us to be happy.

Signed,

Ted, Irma & Charlene

## Contracting with a child-parent

When the recovering child happens to have children of her own, the drawing of lines for a contract can present a painful dilemma. After all, who wants small, innocent grandchildren to be hurt by their parent's dysfunctional behavior?

With that in mind, here is an example of a more formal contract between parents and a recovering daughter who is divorced and caring for two children. As in a legal contract, both the parents and the daughter signed this contract, verifying their consent to its terms:

I, Tom, your father, and I, Mary, your mother, love you and want to continue our relationship with you, Susan, our daughter. We will no longer participate in your addiction, however, and therefore set these limits on ourselves:

1.  We are willing to care for your children once a week, but we will not take care of them for extended periods when you are too intoxicated to do it yourself (such as on your past weekend

binges). If you neglect or abuse the children, we will be forced to inform the proper authorities.

2. We will no longer give you money, outside of gifts at Christmas, birthdays, or other special occasions. We will pay directly for your children's day care, but will not give you money for mortgage payments, car payments, etc.

3. We have paid for your treatment, but will pay for no other treatment in the hospital or any other treatment center. We also have allocated $800 for continued sessions with your counselor, but will give no other money for the treatment of your chemical dependence.

4. We, ourselves, are receiving counseling for our codependence. We are committed to healthy behavior, both in your life and in ours.

A family contract provides a concrete tool for setting limits on the addicted family member as well as on the codependence of those around the addicted and recovering individual. If written with great care it can be very effective.

If the contract is being written between parents and a teenager (minor), careful consideration must be given to parental responsibilities for the underage child. Certainly, if the child is threatening harm to self or others or is very ill and requires medical attention, the parents will need to intervene. Such stipulations can be written into the contract.

The previous samples, of course, represent only two of many ways in which a contract may be written. Each family has different needs, so each contract must be tailored to fit the special circumstances. The main goal in a contract is defining responsibility. When each person knows what to expect of the other, the family will have made great strides toward healthy living.

# *Reflections*

Practice writing a contract for your family. Start by stating how much you love your child and why. Then specify your goals and your limitations. You will probably need assistance as you write the contract, but practicing will allow you to think about the things you want to say.

After writing a contract, even in rough form, share it with your spouse or another family member affected by your child's behavior. (If you find it difficult to share this with another family member, you may need further help from a professional counselor to get everyone to discuss the family problem.)

# Rediscovering Life: The Parental Grief Process

---

*If Winter comes, can Spring be far behind?*

—Percy Bysshe Shelley, "Ode to the West Wind"

---

Blair had just celebrated one year of sobriety with her friends at AA. Ted, her father, was close on her heels with over ten months of sobriety. But things were looking a bit shaky; Ted and Irma were back in my office for a marital therapy session.

**Irma:** *We came to see you because we've been going through hard times. It got so bad that Ted even moved out of the house for a few months.*

**Ted:** *We thought this part of our lives would be easier, once both Blair and I had started recovery. But we were wrong. This last year has been the hardest. We've been fighting a great deal.*

**Irma:** *And I've been attending the meetings to help me overcome the codependence. But I have to tell you, I'm depressed. I also have a deep sense of anger that just won't go away. How can I get over this depression?*

**Farris:** *I know you've been going through great change in your lives. And I want you to be encouraged by the progress you've made. I realize it's difficult to face the recovery of one person in the family, but you are facing the recovery of two people from chemical dependence. And really, each of you is recovering. You know what I mean. You're recovering from family codependence. Irma, I think you are feeling it the most.*

**Irma:** *You're right. They have their AA meetings and therapy groups for continuing care. I feel I have nothing. Just a big hole in my life. I don't know why I can't get over this. I feel as if I have no purpose, and can't find one.*

**Farris:** *You're both going through grief. Ted, you, like Blair, have lost the comfort of drugs and alcohol. Even though the addiction had its price, it also supplied the comfort of helping each of you drop out of the world through alcohol or drugs.*

*In addition, both of you are going through another grief—the loss of parenthood. Oh, you're still parents, but it's different now. You were caring for a little girl who refused to grow up. Her addiction kept her irresponsible and you continued to run her life. Now that is over. She no longer needs you in that way. She needs you in a different way. She loves you in a different way.*

*But that doesn't make the change any easier. You're still grieving a major loss. Your world centered upon her. Now that is gone. It's a new world and you have to face grieving the loss and creating a new life, just as truly as Blair must create a new life of sobriety.*

**Irma:** *But where do we start? I'm tired of feeling so empty and sad.*

**Farris:** *I'd like to help you start the process by looking at some positive things. Try to remember all the positive things about raising your children. Spend some time talking about all the good experiences you had with them. In this way you can move on, knowing that the past wasn't just hard times, and that you are moving ahead from some very fulfilling memories.*

**Ted:** *I'm glad you said that. I know it wasn't all bad, even if I was drinking. In the beginning we had a lot of good times. I think we were happy—not necessarily all the time, but a good deal of the time. It's just that the drinking got worse as the years rolled by.*

**Irma:** *We were happy. I remember going on picnics when Blair was a baby. Those were happy times.*

**Farris:** *Then let's begin to talk about those times.*

## Mourning the loss of codependence

When children entrenched in addictive behavior become healthier, they grow less dependent on their parents and more responsible for their own behavior. They become more able to plan for themselves, to manage their money, and to correctly judge the consequences of their actions. Teenagers or young adults who begin a life of recovery from addiction to alcohol or drugs and the accompanying dysfunctional behavior embrace a lifestyle in which they work, attend school, borrow less money from their family, display moral responsibility, and pursue goals.

Initially parents are happy that their child has changed. This is, after all, what they have hoped for and dreamed about—sometimes for years. But when their child begins to progress through recovery they find rising within themselves new feelings of resentment at the "loss" of their child. Though this may seem peculiar, it proves true in almost every case.

As their child makes steps of recovery that lead to a healthier, more productive life, the child is now more self-directed and probably spends less time around the house. The parents' mental picture of a happy family doing things together may not be materializing—even though the child has abandoned the alcohol and drugs. That child is now involved in other things. He may be attending school, working, going to self-help meetings, making new friends, traveling, and even starting his own family (or becoming more involved with his family, if already married).

A child who has been living at home may move out once he has gained enough money and sobriety. An adult child who returned home during addiction may no longer need to be at home, and thus, if married, may return to his spouse and child or, if unmarried, simply move back into his own home.

As parents realize they no longer are needed as much by their child, they also realize that they cannot control their child's life. In vain they had attempted to control his life when he was in the midst of drug addiction or alcoholism, and found it impossible to stop him from using drugs or drinking; yet they still tried to control some aspects of his life, such as codependent control of money, by loaning or giving funds when he needed it. Such control was shaky, at best, and never produced the desired results. The child ultimately did not stop using drugs and alcohol.

But once in recovery a child's need for the parents decreases. And soon the parents discover they need their child more than he needs them. They need to be needed. Their lives were so involved in helping the child, in saving him from the hellish life of addiction, that they often neglected their own lives. Each paid little attention to relationships with their spouse and other family members, to personal interests and pursuits, and even to personal health and appearance. They even may have ignored their own addiction issues.

Like addiction, codependence is a compulsion that ends tragically unless it is confronted and changed. It can be changed as a codependent goes through his own recovery process, which includes facing the loss of the codependent behavior and the "old" life of focusing on others.

When parents face the loss of codependent behavior they must pass through a grieving process. This process is very important. If the codependent does not change, he will ultimately find another person with whom to be codependent, usually another family member. The grieving process through which a parent must pass consists of five parts.

# The steps of parental grieving

## 1. Grieving the loss of my "little child"

Predictably, parents remember a child as little, even though the child has grown into adulthood. This affection is healthy and normal unless it is accompanied by attempts to treat the grown son or daughter as one who still needs protection from the influences of the world. Therefore, the first loss parents must face is the realization that the child is no longer little and helpless.

Emotionally stunted by the use of drugs and alcohol, the child adopts an immature, dependent style similar to that of a little child. True recovery ends this style of life, however, and often makes it difficult for parents to realize they are no longer needed as parents *in that way.* They therefore must release this part of their lives.

This is a grief that, once experienced, must be left behind. This can be accomplished through therapy, self-help groups, and even the listening ears of family members or a spouse who might be passing through the same experience.

## 2. Grieving the loss of my own youth

A child's maturation into adulthood tends to threaten the parents by reminding them that they are growing older. They often fight this tendency by holding on to a child in ways that make the child dependent on them and irresponsible for his own life. This tendency must be confronted, then grieved, in order to let go.

Busy raising their children for twenty to thirty years, parents are absorbed by family matters, their lives filled with concern for their children. Not surprisingly, they are shocked when the grown children become so busy with their own lives that they have little time to spend with their parents. This is doubly true when a child is recovering.

A recovering child often has much catching up to do. The child thus spends a great deal of time in school, at work, and with new relationships. The parents suddenly experience an "empty nest" feeling, reminding them that they, too, have entered a new stage of life. This feeling is threatening only if seen as a loss. If they, instead, consciously grieve the loss of their own youth, they will be free to look ahead to new experiences and perhaps an even more fulfilling phase of life.

## 3. Finding my own "inner child"

When a parent begins the process of letting go of a child, she also begins the process of finding the lost joy of youth. For years that parent has borne the yoke of responsibility for the family, with little or no time to be carefree and adventurous. The parent has, in so doing, lost the experience of "fun."

For the codependent parent, breaking free to rediscover her inner child is a very difficult task, because the seriousness of life has been overwhelming and an overbearing sense of responsibility has dominated the parent's life. The parent may have difficulty joining any group dedicated to a special interest. Whether that special interest be politics, art, travel, or something else, the parent will, at first, be uncomfortable, overcome by a feeling of not fitting in.

Rather than succumbing to the feeling and avoiding such groups, the parent should be patient. As the parent allows time to pass, she will begin to identify with a new role of just being herself again rather than having to be "Mom" (or in the case of a father, "Dad").

## 4. Dealing with other codependencies

Parents will be tempted to switch codependency to another child or find a new arena in which to be super-responsible, such as in the workplace (by becoming a workaholic). This is a way to avoid the process of grief and change. It is also a way to avoid intimacy with their spouse and true peace with themselves. However, it is not effective. Neither is it healthy, for it prevents the parent from moving on in life.

Parents will do better by realizing their need to create a new life less dependent on being a parent. By doing this they free themselves to return to concerns that may have been forsaken long ago in favor of the commitment to family matters.

## 5. Creating a new life for myself

Free from the shackles of codependency, parents can now rediscover the joy of life. They will unearth emotions long buried under codependent anger and disappointment. They will find new desires and new opportunities for living their own lives and for being good to themselves. They may rediscover their marital relationship.

Putting the emotional spotlight on marriage may be painful, especially if the child's dysfunction seemed to be the only interest the parents had in common. Such a couple probably will need marital therapy to help them explore what happened and where they choose to go in their relationship. This can be a difficult part of abandoning a codependent lifestyle. The rewards, however, are great as each spouse discovers a new sense of freedom and new possibilities for the enjoyment of life.

# *Reflections*

In this book's introduction you read a prayer for parents based on the Alcoholics Anonymous "Serenity Prayer." Now I am placing the original before you. It is a prayer about yourself as a recovering person rather than as a parent. Pray it with a focus on your own life, no one else's.

*God, grant me*
*The Serenity to accept the things I cannot change;*
*The Courage to change the things I can;*
*And the Wisdom to know the difference.*

—The "Big Book" of Alcoholics Anonymous

# Getting Better: The Path to Recovery from Codependence

*Therefore do not be anxious about tomorrow, for tomorrow will be anxious for itself. Let the day's own trouble be sufficient for the day.*

—Matthew 6:34

Rebecca appeared to be destined for a successful career. She always did well in school. And after graduating from the local community college she secured a good job as a graphic artist in a large firm. There she met Shane.

Shane was also a graphic artist, but he had held many jobs before this one. After only five months in his current job he already seemed restless.

Shane asked Rebecca to go out with him, and after a few dates they began living together—and using drugs together. Rebecca had tried cocaine and marijuana before meeting Shane, but he introduced her to heroine. When she expressed fear of using the drug, he grew angry. He wanted them to use it together.

# The beginning of sorrows

Soon Shane had an opportunity for a job in another state, so Rebecca moved with him. Lonely for her family, she occasionally visited them, but Shane became very angry when she went to her parents' house. He knew her parents resented him.

During the next three years Rebecca and Shane had two children. Rebecca managed to stay off the drugs during most of each pregnancy, but she quickly returned to the drugs after each baby was born.

Struggling under their growing financial burden, the couple soon ran out of money. Rebecca called her parents, begging for enough cash to pay the rent and feed the babies. They sent the money. Shane, however, used some of it for drugs, and soon it was gone. Rebecca's parents begged her to come home with the children. They would even accept Shane in the house. Shane thought it was a good idea, so they moved into her parents' home.

Shane found no work, and soon tensions in the house soared. In addition, he and Rebecca continued to use drugs secretly. Finally, after two fights with Rebecca's parents, Shane decided to leave. He wanted Rebecca to accompany him, so he threatened to abandon her if she stayed with her parents. She relented and they stole away at night, leaving their babies with Rebecca's parents.

After a week Rebecca returned and entreated her mother to care for the babies for a few days so she could go back to Shane and persuade him to settle down and secure a job. Rebecca then disappeared for six months. During that time she and Shane decided to marry.

When Rebecca finally returned, Shane came with her. Shane's parents had paid for him to enter a drug treatment program, and now Rebecca was imploring her parents to do the same for her. She contended that if both of them got off the drugs, they would live a normal and healthy life. Her parents consented.

During the treatment Rebecca told her counselors of the "six months in hell" she had spent with Shane before coming for treatment. Quickly running out of money, they had attempted everything from theft to prostitution to make enough to live and to buy drugs. Rebecca was exhausted by the experience. Already thin, she had lost fifteen pounds during the ordeal. She was glad to be "clean and sober." When the treatment program ended, however, Rebecca's struggle did not.

Sober again, Shane found a job at a liquor store. Rebecca wanted to find a job as well but also wanted to spend time with her babies—she had missed them immensely during her time with Shane and during her treatment. Shane started to use drugs again and soon lost the liquor store job. After two jobless weeks he left the house. Now Rebecca started to use drugs again. She also started going out with Eric, a man she had met in the treatment center.

## Time for intervention

At this point, after learning of my work at a codependent parents' group they attended, Rebecca's parents sought my help. At their first visit in my office Pat and John were frightened and fed up.

After they explained the situation I advised that they make a contract with Rebecca. I also suggested that Shane's parents be present so all of them would participate in the contract. This contract would outline what the parents of each child would do, and not do, for Rebecca and Shane.

Pat and John agreed to give Rebecca a fixed amount of money each month to help with the care of the children. They would continue financial and emotional support only if she followed an after-care treatment program that included twice-weekly Narcotics Anonymous meetings. They stipulated that she follow this for one year if she wanted their support.

In addition, they would supply no more than the fixed amount, and, should Rebecca revert to using drugs, they would seek to have the children transferred from her custody. The money would stop completely if she relapsed.

## Facing codependence

This contract was Pat and John's way of addressing their own codependence. Once the problem and response had been defined, they stopped their usual arguments and their attempts at controlling Rebecca. They also stopped the ceaseless funding of both her life and her repeated drug treatment programs. They set limits on their need to control her life—their need to change her in order to feel successful as parents.

Pat and John had come to therapy seeking help for Rebecca but soon understood that they really were coming for themselves. They recognized self-defeating attitudes and actions in their relationship with their daughter and her husband. They realized they were not accomplishing their goals with Rebecca because they had become locked in patterns with her that perpetuated the problem. They had always supplied the time, money, energy, and patience that allowed Rebecca to continue using drugs and to continue all of her drug-related behavior.

Pat and John exercised a great measure of courage by admitting they were part of the problem. But it was this admission that allowed them to begin the process of change. They began discussing how to behave toward Rebecca when she used drugs or when she acted irresponsibly in other ways. They also confronted their own past in order to comprehend why they had adopted such patterns of behavior.

Rebecca's father looked at his own painful past of growing up with an abusive father. John had learned to avoid problems in order to survive within such a situation. He also talked about his life when he was Rebecca's age, admitting irresponsibility in leaving his first wife with two children and not contributing to their welfare for three years.

Pat discussed her childhood with an alcoholic father and her ambivalent feelings toward him. She loved him yet hated him. Only later could she understand how she could love and hate at the same time.

Pat now perceived that she had the same feelings toward Rebecca, because of Rebecca's drug use. Rather than feeling guilty about her feelings after discovering this, she allowed herself to feel both love and hate for Rebecca. This admission of her feelings allowed Pat to choose her response to Rebecca rather than reacting to her guilt over love and hate.

As they progressed, Pat and John learned to bare these feelings to each other. Previously they shared only their anxiety; each was afraid to talk about the other feelings from their past. Now they felt more free, after discussing these matters in therapy sessions, to share about themselves and to make decisions together about their response to Rebecca. It was a brand new experience for them.

Previously Pat and John often blamed each other for giving in to Rebecca or for driving her away by being too harsh. Now they were preparing together for the things they feared—Rebecca's relapse or other irresponsible behavior—and deciding how to face each scenario. This was a milestone in their lives. They had found the key to shifting responsibility back to Rebecca for her own life.

# Signs of recovery from codependence

"How will I know I'm getting better and not being so codependent?" It's a common question posed by parents like Pat and John. The answer, unfortunately, is not simple.

The reason for this difficulty? Parents are often so detached from their feelings and so unaware of their own needs that they cannot tell the difference between normal and codependent behavior. They may even wonder if a simple act, such as giving a birthday present, is codependent. There is no clear answer; such an act may be performed in a manipulative fashion or because of a sense of guilt, or it may be done out of untainted love.

The following five hallmarks provide a good measurement of recovery from codependence and of change to a lifestyle of freedom and healthy love.

### 1. The codependent individual begins to focus on his own life instead of the life of the addicted person

The codependent person no longer adjusts his schedule around that of the addicted person. He no longer makes adjustments out of guilt or makes decisions based solely on the reaction of the addicted family member. He now trusts his own intuition and judgment and does not allow others to take advantage of him.

### 2. The codependent person no longer takes inappropriate responsibility for others

There is no longer a feeling of having to "take up the slack" for another, a feeling that "if I don't do it, no one else will." Although this will require those around the codependent person to experience the consequences of his irresponsibility, and thus suffer from this, the codependent person realizes that this will be the only way in which the others will grow up.

Allowing others to be responsible will be difficult because it means letting things happen and not rescuing the family. But the reward will be great: freedom from the tremendous responsibility.

### 3. The codependent person develops new interests

With focus back on the self, codependent persons now begin to feel new desires, develop new interests, and set new goals. They may thus pursue a new life, new friends, or a new career.

Once codependent behavior is released, there is also more time to do these things whereas previously so much time was consumed bearing the responsibility of others. Now there is time to "pursue my life again," because others are expected to do the things that are their responsibility.

### 4. The codependent person begins to address his own addictive behavior

Often codependence is a mask for problems of addiction to alcohol, drugs, overeating, gambling, tobacco, or sex. The codependent person used the addicted person to avoid dealing with such problems, thus practicing a strong form of denial.

Such addictive behavior frequently is dismissed through such statements as: "I'm not the problem—my son was the one arrested for driving under the influence of alcohol," or "I can handle my beer, but it's my daughter's use of drugs that is the real problem." When such statements disappear and the codependent person begins to address his own dependencies, recovery takes a giant leap forward.

### 5. The codependent person discovers a sense of joy

Joy is the spiritual quality of losing oneself in the pleasure of the moment. Codependents cannot experience this because they have lost the ability to relax and to have fun. They cannot be spontaneous, for they feel always responsible. Joy in friendships, in work, in travel, and in hobbies or pet projects are examples of the signs of recovery from codependence.

The individual discovers the joy of the moment when he "lets go and lets God." He stops trying to control the world around him and experiences the pleasure of life. He experiences the pleasure of being with those he loves without trying to always protect or control them. He experiences the pleasure of liking and loving himself—of realizing the gift of life that he has been given, and breathing easier as he enjoys that gift.

# *Reflections*

*Take life too seriously and what is it worth? If the morning wake us to no new joys, if the evening bring us not the hope of new pleasures, is it worthwhile to dress and undress? Does the sun shine on me today that I may reflect on yesterday? That I may endeavor to foresee and to control what can neither be foreseen nor controlled—the destiny of tomorrow?*

—Goethe

1. Look again at the story of Rebecca and her parents, then take a sheet of paper and write your own story. It need not be long, but write enough so you can compare your life with that of the story recounted in this chapter.

2. What signs of codependence do you see in your own life that parallel the experience of Rebecca's parents?

3. Which, if any, of the five hallmarks of recovery are evident in your life? Which seem, at this time, most impossible to achieve?

# PART THREE

# Understanding the Adolescent Child

# The Child Who Is No Longer a Child: The Changes of Adolescence

---

*I don't understand her. I say the same thing
at two different times of the day and I get two exactly
opposite responses. She sometimes seems
like two people in one body.*
—Mother of a teenage girl

*I try to teach them logical thinking,
but I really don't believe that they can think logically—
at least, not like an adult thinks.*
—A high school teacher

---

Accoording to Erik Erikson, the focus of adolescence is a struggle to establish identity amid role confusion. Adolescents strive to define their identities and roles in the sexual and career areas of their lives (as well as class or ethnic roles) during this first stage of breaking their identification with the family (a twenty-year process after adolescence). If they do not succeed in establishing their identities, they are very confused about future roles.

Amid their struggle to establish an identity adolescents can be devastated by the abuse of drugs or alcohol. This is because addiction, and the denial that attends it, causes identity confusion. (While addicted people really are addicted, they generally deny their identity as an addicted person until they recognize that the dysfunction in their lives is related to the use of drugs or alcohol.)

Adolescents also are seeking to identify with a group of people in order to confirm their own identity. Thus, when they link their identity with others who are addicted their self-concept adapts in such a way that change becomes very difficult—they have no healthy identity to which they can return.

Chemical addiction in adolescence also skews the person's view of "normalcy." Already unclear about identity, then becoming addicted, such a person is greatly perplexed as to how life could be any different or better. Having never experienced a normal, addiction-free identity, such individuals aren't sure what they should become when faced with the need to change. In attempting to return to normalcy and leave the addictive behavior, they wonder what "normal" is, for they have never experienced a normal adult identity.

# Physical change

In addition to their identity conflicts, adolescents are facing other immense upheavals in their bodies. Puberty, for instance, brings physical changes that cause stress for their physical systems as well as their social systems. These physical changes include hormonal changes, abrupt growth, and high energy levels.

## Hormonal changes

As teenagers grow, the chemistry of their bodies transforms in amazing ways as hormones initiate an array of secondary sexual characteristics. Boys gain facial and bodily hair, a more masculine shape, and a deeper voice. Girls develop breasts (requiring brassieres as a new part of their wardrobe), wider hips, and a monthly cycle of fertility.

Such sexual development gives rise to a new interest in the opposite sex. With this new interest, however, come also the hopes and fears of the future, the anxiety over being accepted or rejected, and the wonderment at the experience of sexual pleasure itself.

## Abrupt growth

Growth comes in spurts for the teenager. It is not always a smooth, elegant process as certain systems of the body may grow at a faster pace than others. Adolescents must adapt to this body that is becoming larger—and different. This often makes adolescents seem gangly and awkward as they become accustomed to larger bodies. At the same time, hormonal changes provoke a restyled bone structure in the face, replacing the soft face of childhood with the defined adult face of a man or woman. Thus, the poor adolescent may be klutzing about like a toddler while looking like an adult.

## High energy levels

During adolescence the cardiopulmonary system, the heart and lungs, increases its capacity to process the flow of blood and the intake of oxygen as well as to eliminate toxins and nonuseful materials. This increase in the capacity of the cardiopulmonary system allows the teenager to endure prolonged periods of exercise or exertion without the need for equivalent periods of rest.

Although their recovery (from exercise) period is shortened because of this increased capacity, this does not mean teenagers need little or no rest at night. Rather, it means they can experience more activity without rest between periods of exertion.

Due to this high energy level, the effects of drug or alcohol use seem less extreme to the adolescent. The person recovers faster from the effects of the substances, thus building a false sense of invulnerability to drugs and alcohol. Even if teenagers feel intoxicated or sick from the use of chemicals, the physical effects seem more moderate than the effects on a person the age of their parents.

# Emotional change

In concert with the overt physical changes a teenager experiences are the more subtle, though sometimes glaring, behavioral changes that arise from evolving self-esteem, egocentrism, and identity and a sense of immortality. In their quest for maturity adolescents reveal their attitudes and approaches to these concerns by the way they act.

## Self-esteem

Teenagers are very pliable. Seeking approval from others, especially from peers, they tend to be nonassertive when faced with predicaments in which they need to be assertive. Such was the case in the Just Say No program promoted in the 1980s by the Reagan administration. Adolescents were encouraged to "just say no" to drugs and alcohol offered to them by others. The campaign, however, failed to provide a way for teens to be assertive enough to just say no. Teenagers face intense pressure to say yes to practically anything their peers ask them to do.

Teenagers are more easily pressured than adults into going along with the crowd. After all, they want to become one of the group, their crowd of peers. They want to build a sense of self-esteem separate from their identification with their own childhood and family life.

Part of the search for self-esteem includes being "sophisticated." Too often drugs and alcohol are seen as a part of this sophistication. Not wishing to appear naive in any of these matters, they experiment with drugs, take risks, and attempt sexual behaviors.

In their striving for self-esteem, adolescents also seek role models—heroes. By modeling themselves after people considered strong, popular, beautiful, and successful they gain a measure of self-esteem. As they hear the stories of others, they try unconsciously to create their own story, their own identity. They also formulate a goal—adulthood—and to reach that goal they devise a means, the way to grow up. The goal is not just adulthood, but adulthood that they consider "successful."

This "success," of course, is from an adolescent point of view. It may thus mean rejecting their own parents as role models in order to be a separate person. Adolescents do not want to be identified as so-and-so's son or daughter. Even if parents are strong, successful, beautiful, and popular, teenagers tend to reject them as role models out of a desire to establish a separate identity.

This is also time for mood swings as teenagers experience new pain, disappointments, successes, feelings, and understandings. This newness comes as they attempt to adopt new roles of adulthood and discard the old roles of childhood.

Sometimes this process does not end during adolescence. Young adults who do not develop adult coping skills and a relatively healthy style of life may continually revert to old emotional responses in both happy and sad experiences. They therefore will not act as adults but will continue to celebrate and grieve as adolescents.

## Egocentrism

Teenagers overestimate their significance to others. They believe the world revolves around their actions and that it should revolve around their desires. Adolescents are, therefore, very self-conscious in public, acting as if on stage when they are with others. When alone they will create an imaginary audience as they fantasize about the reactions of others.

Sometimes teens, in their terrible self-consciousness, do rude or silly things to overcome tension or embarrassment. These things may include making strange noises, mimicking people they are with, and unleashing outbursts of laughter.

Such antics seem obnoxious to parents but usually are harmless, and they even may be healthy. These high-energy teens are simply responding to pressure they feel from all of the potent changes transforming them from children to adults. They purposely divert public attention to their apparently absurd behavior rather than be judged for attempts at "grown-up" behavior. In this way they can control a situation. Even if public opinion goes against them, at least they have forced the issue and don't have to spend time nervously awaiting judgment. It's over and done with and the tension has passed. It's finished.

As part of their egocentrism teenagers also fantasize about their future. They imagine grand and glorious deeds as they spend hours daydreaming about being a star athlete, film celebrity, brilliant doctor, successful model, popular musician, or one of a thousand other careers and roles in our society. And the choice of careers and roles may change as the adolescents meet new adults or hear of other lives, then imagine themselves in yet other adult roles.

## Group identity

Adolescents long to be part of a group, yet they often lack enough self-confidence to be individuals in taste and opinion. This pursuit of identity with a group is part of the search for an identity. As they discover an identity adolescents grow in confidence, especially in confidence about their own ideas and the ability to trust their feelings. This growth allows them to become individuals.

If drugs enter the picture the process of individuation becomes retarded. This is because the drugs cause the teenager to lose touch with feelings and sound judgment. They therefore lack trust of their own ideas and allow the group to retain control. In such a situation the adolescent is unable to create a personal identity.

When drugs have made the group's dominance even stronger, the individual does not develop "will power," which is normally the product of identity. If that teenager attempts recovery, eliminating this aspect of the addiction process will be extremely difficult. He probably will endure a great struggle to reject the old group of drug-using friends and to establish both a strong personal identity and a new circle of friends with strong and healthy identities.

Sampling a new identity may sometimes require acting out in an antisocial fashion. This is a way of testing the limits of social approval as well as peer approval. These attempts at a new identity include rites of initiation and passage, as sanctioned by various groups and subgroups of our culture. Identity, of course, comes from affiliation with groups, such as the football team, the cheerleading squad, the "brainy group," the drama group, and so on. But often drugs and alcohol are used as initiation into such groups (such as when the group invites a new member to a party where everyone is expected to get drunk).

Substance abuse also may be a continued test of loyalty to the group: the teenager who stops drinking or using drugs will be snubbed by the group, even if still formally a member. The football player who won't get drunk at the party after the game will still be on the football team but will be ostracized by the other team members—not because of performance during the game or practice, but because of nonperformance at the celebration after the game.

Such impossible pressure usually forces the adolescent to desert the program that this group represents. For example, the drama club member who abstains from drugs yet is expected by peers to use drugs with them will drop out of the drama club and probably forsake all dramatic productions as well.

The importance of finding an identity through the group is so strong that anyone who becomes strong enough to reject drugs or alcohol is viewed as a threat to the group. Group leaders, who find both identity and power in the group, will feel the greatest threat and thus will react quickly to ostracize the person.

## Immortality

Adolescents believe themselves immune from matters such as pregnancy and arrest. When such an event does strike their lives, they react in shock—"I can't believe this is happening to me!" This is also the case in drug use. A teenager almost always finds it impossible to believe he is "addicted" to a drug. This is a part of the denial system that fits neatly into addiction denial.

Denial of a negative circumstance, which is natural for a teenager, accompanies the belief that "I will live forever." Death and danger seem far away, because for most teenagers, they are. But this feeling, of course, gives a false sense of security and a distorted sense of reality. Dangerous stunts, gang violence, and unsafe sexual experiences don't seem to carry any threat of injury, disease, or death. The person, during the teenage years, enjoys a sense of being above life and its dangers.

This denial is also a factor in attempted suicide among teens, especially when combined with the previous factor of egocentrism and the limited ability to make sound judgments. An adolescent may weigh suicide as a means to show friends or parents how much pain he has inflicted on the individual. He rarely fathoms that a suicide attempt may actually result in death.

This is the ultimate result of the false sense of immortality. Death seems so distant that even the thought of suicide does not equal death. Such a lack of sound judgment, joined with a sense of immortality, equals suicide risk—and the risk is doubled when drugs are involved. Drugs reduce what little sound judgment exists and heighten the sense of being above life, of being immune to reality and death.

# Intellectual change

Research shows that teenagers are able to build systems of thought, or theories. This is significant for adolescents, for they are now able to understand the logical consequences of actions and choices. They also no longer must learn only from trial and error or from the reward and punishment system maintained by those in authority.

Equipped with such intellectual powers teenagers begin to speculate on ethical issues. They learn to think for themselves without appealing to authority. They no longer do—or not do—something simply because a parent, teacher, or minister says it is right or wrong. This sometimes gets them into trouble, because their ability to think for themselves is yet unfinished. For this reason we appropriately call the fifteen-year-old a "sophomore"—which comes from the Greek words *sophos* and *moros*, meaning "wise fool."

Parents of a fifteen-year-old adolescent are often shocked, or at least very concerned, because their child is trying out new ideas. Such children may, for a while, tout themselves as atheists, simply to exercise independence from their parents' beliefs. They may acquire ideas opposite of their parents' just for shock value. They also may do it because they enjoy the feeling of thinking different ideas, of finding their own beliefs as they stretch their newly acquired mental muscles for abstract thinking.

This ability, and these new ideas, may scare the adolescents themselves. Although they may act grown up, they still do not feel independent and grown up. They wish to stand apart from their parents but nonetheless lack the experience and self-confidence to do so. Standing independently with their ideas is an effective way to enjoy a sense of independence without leaving home.

In itself this phase of independent thought should not alarm parents. Rather than responding with defensiveness they can seize the opportunity for dialogue. They can say to their child, "I see your point, let's talk about it." Rather than creating conflict over religious beliefs, politics, sexuality, and so on, such a response allows the parents to fully discuss their beliefs with their child and to present their values without having to stand on a soapbox.

Such personal values are very important to the teenager at this time of growth because each adolescent is seeking to be a whole person. They want to have their own feelings and thoughts and formulate their own decisions and values. Parents can impart true wisdom during this time of adolescence if they allow their child the freedom to choose ideas rather than forcing that child to accept the parents' value system. Any attempt at such force almost always fails.

# *Reflections*

1. List some of the ways your adolescent child has changed—physically, emotionally, and intellectually—in the past five years. How have these changes affected your relationship with that child?

2. Try to recall your own adolescence. What were two of the most significant events in your teen years? Who were your heroes or idols in your teen years? What were your fantasies as a teenager?

3. Did you have a favorite political or religious belief that you liked to defend as a teenager? Do you still believe that way?

4. Does your son or daughter espouse views that clash with your own? Do you argue about these views?

5. How does your teenager think like you?

# Drugs and Your Teenager

*I do not understand my own actions. For I do not do what I want, but I do the very thing I hate.*

—Romans 7:15

When it comes to drugs, adolescents are unique. This is because drugs affect an adolescent more severely than they affect an adult. Drugs disturb the already unstable state of adolescent growth by (1) retarding emotional development; (2) lowering inhibitions against behavior that a teenager might avoid if drug-free; and (3) increasing the natural tendency toward egocentrism.

## Drugs retard emotional development

Drugs do this by dulling the emotions. Both old and new feelings become lost to the individual when using drugs. It is often said that drug-addicted people act like teenagers, no matter what age they are. This frequently is true, because drugs tend to freeze emotional progress at the age level in which the individual began to take the drugs.

Doctors often use medications to alter emotions—to elevate or tranquilize moods. The same thing happens when a person self-medicates through drug abuse. They suspend emotional growth.

It is very hard for an adolescent, while under the influence of drugs, to experience feelings of affection, hope, fear, and triumph. Some of these are new feelings, contents of the individual's adolescent "package." If, rather than being experienced, the feelings are repressed and distorted by drugs, the teenager does not grow but becomes fixed in adolescence. New growth probably will come only through recovery.

Meanwhile, adolescents learn to distrust feelings because their feelings often prove to be inappropriate or because they feel numb or angry most of the time. This mistrust of feelings translates into mistrust of others as teenagers meet with (perceived) betrayal from those they love. Love from family members and friends seems inconsistent, after all, with teenagers' antisocial behavior. Teenagers therefore love parents, siblings, other relatives, and friends but now can no longer trust them, because no one is to be trusted. Teenagers enter a world of fear and suspicion.

Through the eyes of the drug-addicted teenager, the feelings that drugs provide are the only ones that seem real—and all of the rest are not to be trusted if they interfere with the ability to use drugs. Adolescents are thus in an awful predicament. They cannot trust parents, teachers, or counselors. They cannot trust friends. They cannot trust their own feelings.

This predicament is illustrated by the case of Baxter, a tall, thin sixteen-year-old boy with curly dark hair. Until a sophomore he had played basketball for the school team, but during that year he began to use drugs. He missed many practices and soon lost the motivation to stay on the team.

Baxter's parents, extremely upset about these developments, brought him to my office. Baxter was quiet and polite to me but critical of his mother during our family sessions. In private sessions he also talked with me, but I sensed an emotional wall separating us. That wall, I realized, was *honesty*. Baxter was unable to be honest with his parents, who seemed threatening to him. Neither was he able to be honest with me, though I had made clear my desire to help him. Our dialogue went like this:

**Farris:** *I want to tell you two things. First, I am against the use of drugs—by you or anyone. Second, I will not attempt to change* *your decision to use drugs. You must decide that you want to change. If you do, I will be there to help. Until then, you may come to see me and be honest about drug use. I will be here for you regardless of what you do.*

**Baxter:** *But I don't use very much.*

**Farris:** *Baxter, I don't believe that—in the face of your low grades, dropping out of school sports, and your parents' report on your mood swings and change in friends.*

**Baxter:** *You think I'm lying!*

**Farris:** *I think you are telling me that you don't want my help right now. When you do, I'll be available. Here's my business card. Call me when you are ready. Okay?*

**Baxter:** *I guess so.*

Baxter dropped out of counseling, much to his parents' disappointment. Yet six months later, when his drug abuse had grown much worse, Baxter did call me. He asked for my help and I put him in a treatment program.

This story has a happy ending, because, at last count, Baxter has been clean and sober for fourteen months. He needed to seek his recovery on his own, and he needed to *choose* to trust again. While his parents and I didn't approve of his drug use, we knew that we couldn't control Baxter's decision to use drugs. Our prayers and his decision to trust again allowed the door of recovery to be opened and Baxter to escape the nightmare of addiction through that door.

# Drugs lower inhibitions

The judgment ability of an adolescent is very immature. And when mixed with drugs, a dangerous situation results. The peril is evident in the risks teenagers normally take, risks that older persons would resist. Teenagers will throw caution to the wind in sexual relations, driving, crime, and chemical abuse. Fused with a sense of immortality, this recklessness can be fatal if it ensues in a suicide attempt, reckless driving, and other such behavior.

The loss of inhibitions through drug abuse also can confuse moral issues for teenagers, who find themselves in sexual situations that may confuse even adults. Teenagers are struggling to find a sexual identity. Drugs, rather than helping, will hinder the process by making matters seem even less clear. Adolescents who enter sexual activities under the influence of drugs may be unclear of their intentions, their sexual orientation, their sexual roles, or even their chosen sexual behavior. From a sexuality standpoint the teen years are already a difficult time, and drugs worsen the difficulty.

A perfect example of the inhibition problem is the experience of a high school freshman named Susan. Excited about boys, she sought hard for their attention. During a spring break, when the weather was particularly warm, a number of students from Susan's school held a beach party. The beach was crowded with young people, and when night fell they lit several fires on the sand and some of the students began to pair off and sit around the fires.

Susan, without a boyfriend, felt a bit depressed. She noticed, however, that four junior boys who had moved down the beach were laughing loudly in the darkness. She followed the sandy path toward the boys and found them drinking beer. Susan began to talk with them and soon they were urging her to walk further with them—and to help them consume the beer.

Susan began to drink and soon found herself enjoying the attention of these older boys. They urged her to perform suggestive acts, including removing her clothes, and soon Susan found herself going beyond anything she would have imagined. Soon after being coaxed into this sexual experience with the four boys, she began to realize this was not what she really wanted. Feeling ashamed and humiliated, she began to cry uncontrollably. The boys grew frightened and ran from the scene, leaving Susan to find her way back to the rest of the partygoers.

Susan's feelings of humiliation did not stop, and she left school for a semester while undergoing therapy. She never returned to that school (but was allowed to attend another school) because she feared facing her school friends after the beach incident. Alcohol, the liquid drug, had so influenced Susan's judgment, as well as the judgment of the four boys, that normal choices were obscured as the confusion of adolescent sexuality was compounded by the blur of intoxication.

# Drugs increase egocentrism

Already focused on self, an adolescent who uses drugs becomes even more self-absorbed as drugs demand more and more attention in caring for oneself. The person's life becomes centered on obtaining the drugs when needed or desired; on hiding the drugs and protecting oneself with lies and avoidance behavior (to elude the observant eyes of family, friends, teachers, and others); on protecting oneself while under the influence of drugs, so as not to be caught. The individual becomes increasingly selfish, increasingly absorbed with personal concerns.

Already struggling to define identity and future roles, an adolescent's egocentrism is compounded by drug use. This grows more precarious as the teenager becomes even more emotionally isolated in the world of the self—a very lonely existence, without the connections of love and trust. This is a sad and terrifying situation for the adolescent and one that causes frustration and pain for family members.

The story of Baxter, which I recounted earlier, comes to mind again. I had stated that six months elapsed between Baxter's decision not to attend counseling sessions and his desperate phone call asking me for help with his drug addiction. During those six months Baxter had entered the terrifying and lonely world of drug dependence.

Although I told you the story had a happy ending, I also will admit that it had some very heartbreaking chapters. For six months Baxter lived with drug-using friends, then finally on the street. His parents lost contact with him. Already thin, he lost an additional sixteen pounds. Broke and sick, alone and scared, he finally called a phone number from the past—my number.

I thank God I was at the other end of the phone line, because, as I stated earlier, I was able to help Baxter by admitting him into a hospital treatment program. Other teen stories have ended in tragedy. This one was a triumph.

# *Reflections*

1.   Do you remember the first time you used alcohol? Drugs? What have you said to your children about this experience? What would you like to say?

2.   Sometimes painful experiences occur between parents and their child because of drug use. Do you remember one such experience between you and your child?

3.   Hope is a necessary part of healing. To heal a rift between you and your teenager, you must begin with the hope that the relationship can be healed. Do you have that hope? If yes, what is the reason for your hope?

# Facing the Drug Whirlwind

*The waters closed in over me,*
*the deep was round about me; weeds were wrapped*
*about my head at the roots of the mountains. I went*
*down to the land whose bars closed upon me forever;*
*yet thou didst bring up my life from the Pit,*
*O LORD my God.*

—Jonah 2:5, 6

Barry and Jeremy had become close friends during Barry's senior year of high school. When Barry had arrived in California from Michigan a year ago, he felt like an outsider, unable to find a group of friends. Being a newcomer, as well as a senior, was tough. Jeremy was also a kind of outsider at school. His friends were all either at other schools or simply no longer attending school.

Barry had no history of drug addiction, although he had tried alcohol and marijuana while living in Michigan. Jeremy, on the contrary, had been using drugs heavily since the age of fourteen. Barry was an average student; Jeremy could not have cared less about grades. (He was now only in his sophomore year of school because of poor grades.) Barry was quiet because he was shy; Jeremy was quiet in a cautious, secretive way. They were, in many ways, an odd couple.

Barry's parents contacted me after discovering the butt of a marijuana cigarette on the floor of the family car. They previously had suspected Barry of drug use but had had no solid evidence. After finding the cigarette, Barry's parents contacted Jeremy's parents because Barry had recently used the car to attend a party with Jeremy and two other boys. Barry had been "grounded" after returning from the party two hours late. For the first visit I urged Jeremy's parents to come in with Barry's parents.

When they arrived, all of the parents were angry. Jeremy's parents were angry because this was simply another chapter in his drug use. They were tired of his behavior and said they were waiting for his eighteenth birthday to force him out of the house.

Barry's parents were angry because of their disappointment with Barry. The couple was recently married—Barry and his mother had moved to California when she decided to marry the man who was now Barry's stepfather. According to the mother, Barry had always been a "good boy" while in Michigan. Now he was changing.

When asked to explain the changes, she said, "Barry was always good in school, and he liked sports. When he came to southern California with me, I thought we'd have a new life together. But instead, things are getting worse." I asked her to describe the changes further.

"Barry seems to be really angry all the time. Then, he apologizes—and sometimes I see him cry. His grades are not as good as before. He used to get along well with his stepfather. Now all they do is argue. I blame myself for taking him away from his friends. He was happy in Michigan."

I responded by explaining that she needed to stop dwelling on her regrets; there was nothing she could do about the past. She could, however, deal with the present. She therefore began, with my help, to outline the changes in Barry's behavior. Here is her list:

| In California | In Michigan |
|---|---|
| Only one friend comes around | Many friends visited |
| No interest in sports | Played football/baseball |
| Always sloppily dressed | Usually neatly dressed |
| Always angry—sometimes cries | Always seemed happy |
| Grades dropping to "D" level | "B" and "C" grades |

Jeremy's parents then entered the conversation. They observed that Barry's mother had given a perfect description of Jeremy's behavior when he was fourteen and starting to use drugs. His behavior was now far worse.

Barry's mother began to cry. Regretting their move to California and worried that Barry's drug use—and behavior—might increase, she moaned, "I'm afraid of the future now. I think he's going to get worse."

## Signs of change

The chemically dependent adolescent may start with casual drug use just to try the experience or because she is pressured by friends. This is even more probable if other members of her family use alcohol or drugs. Initially the drug use may be well concealed, but as use increases, the effect of the drug becomes suprisingly apparent.

As drug use heightens, the teenager decreases her tolerance for frustration and is quickly angered. She no longer pays attention in school and thus loses interest. Soon she is cutting classes and eventually may skip school entirely.

The drug-using teenager may begin to cultivate a new group of friends—fellow drug users. If the crowd is in the habit of wearing distinctive clothing, such as dressing in black or dying their hair, the teenager probably will begin dressing in a similar fashion. School, of course, may have some attraction because of this drug-using crowd, but it also presents the burden of facing school authorities who may question and discipline the student who acts in this way. Grades spiral downward under these circumstances and the student fails.

The adolescent will likely exhibit mood swings ranging from depression to exuberance. These swings will be more extreme than the normal mood swings of adolescence. Her mood may fluctuate throughout the day, according to the rhythm of drug use.

As the drug use increases, interest in other activities usually declines. Hobbies or physical activities may be neglected to the point that there is almost no desire for sports, clubs, and other former interests—unless the activity is somehow related to drugs (for example, drug-related music).

The *need* to use drugs also increases, so the teenager probably will stop attending school. She may be arrested for theft (to procure drug money), for driving under the influence, or even for assault (decreased ability to control anger). The teen's goals and dreams become muddled and she shows little desire to think about the future.

Yet even amid all of this trouble, the drug-abusing teenager will not admit she has a problem. Therefore, if treatment begins, the first difficult task is breaking through the denial of drug use, the natural teenage disbelief that she could be addicted. Help, however, is out of reach until the adolescent honestly confronts the problem of addiction and asks for help.

# Recovering from the drug storm: stages of recovery

With so much emphasis today on identifying the process of addiction among adolescents, identifying the recovery process is often overlooked. It is vital to understand, because the teenager's process of recovery is distinct from that of the adult.

The adolescent's process is unique because, unlike an adult, the growth and formation of personality is not yet solidified. In light of this factor of adolescent growth, the following stages of an adolescent's recovery from addiction provide useful insights.

## Stage one

Adolescents face the futility of assertiveness. As soon as they admit their problem of misusing drugs, teenagers realize that recovery will require more than self-effort, more than just an attempt at abstinence. As with adults in recovery, adolescents must recognize the failure of trying to cure themselves and instead follow a prescribed program of recovery.

## Stage two

Teenagers listen to the stories of others who are addicted. Adolescents have listened often to others' stories because that is part of the (almost) unconscious process of attempting to create an adult identity. Substance abuse, however, has served to confused this process—their unstable, volatile attempts at establishing an identity have been destabilized further by alcohol and drugs.

Adolescents, at this stage, begin treatment by performing self-assessments and also by learning information about chemical dependence. They begin to increase hope for a better life by leaving behind the addictions. Listening to other teenagers aids the creation of one's own story of addiction and recovery.

## Stage three

Just as they are accustomed to listening to stories, adolescents have also been involved in the dynamics of creating an identity by creating a story. To create an identity, we each tell a story of who we are, who our parents are, what we do, what we want to be, what our interests are, and so on. At this point the story of addiction and recovery is added to the complete story, the identity of the adolescent.

By creating their own story, teenagers begin to entertain hopes for a better future, though without specific plans. However, they are still following an external program rather than an internal conviction to change. They may feel little emotional involvement with the recovery process—which will come in stage four.

## Stage four

The most significant attribute of adolescent recovery is the movement from self-absorbed isolation to genuine concern for others. This is also natural for teenagers, who grow enough emotionally to turn from adolescent concerns about self to a concern for others. Drugs and alcohol, of course, had retarded the progress of this process.

This stage begins the building of one's own story *after* treatment. The story of addiction and recovery is now complete enough that the teenager starts progressing to the interests of career and personal relationships. The normal process of maturation, which was halted by drugs, can now resume. The addictive period may even seem like a dream for the recovering teenager, who may think, "Did this really happen to me? Was I really addicted?"

Involvement in a continuing recovery program may be hampered by intense career or relationship demands. This increases the risk of returning to addiction if such activities are actually a form of denial. Although the teenager may not be devastated by a "slip" into alcohol or drug use, she should recognize such a slip as the final warning to return to an intensive program of recovery.

During this stage the teenager will finally focus on an appropriate goal: accomplishing the task of recovery (not on "serenity," the usual goal for recovering adults). For the adolescent, viewing recovery as a task rather than a way of life does not imperil sobriety. That mindset is appropriate to the age of adolescence. The sense of accomplishment that recovery provides is natural to this period of life.

# *Reflections*

*Afflicted and close to death from my youth up,*
*I suffer thy terrors; I am helpless.*
*Thy wrath has swept over me;*
*thy dread assaults destroy me.*
*They surround me like a flood all day long;*
*they close in upon me together.*
*Thou hast caused lover and friend to shun me;*
*my companions are in darkness.*

—Psalms 88:15-18

1. This passage from the Psalms is a fitting description of "hitting bottom." It may be the experience of your adolescent child. When, and in what ways, have you felt their pain as well as your own frustration and anger?

*Ah! Up then from the ground sprang I*
*And hailed the earth with such a cry*
*As is not heard save from a man*
*Who has been dead and lives again.*

—Edna St. Vincent Millay, "Renascence"

2. The child you once knew seems so different under the influence of these drugs or alcohol. What changes have taken place during your child's time of chemical abuse?

3. If your child has begun the recovery process, do you see a different peron emerging? What are the differences? What remains, as yet, unchanged?

# *Involved, but Not Involved: Knowing Your Limits*

*Weep not, child,*
*Weep not, my darling,*
*With these kisses let me remove your tears.*

—Walt Whitman, "On the Beach at Night"

Because adolescents are under the age of legal adulthood, their parents have more difficulty knowing the limits of responsibility than do the parents of adult children. Parents of a minor are still responsible for the child's actions until that child is either of legal age or is emancipated by the court.

Parents should realize, however, that they may be acting in codependent fashion when they prevent their child from facing the consequences of one's actions. (An adolescent child can quickly learn that productive actions reap benefits while irresponsible and harmful actions reap pain.) Parents can begin to assess their level of codependence by asking, "Is my child's behavior harming my own life or the life of my family? And is that behavior detracting from the success and welfare of my family?"

# Building an environment for recovery

## Assist, don't force

If a parent answers yes to the above questions, the next step is to ask, "How can I *assist* my child in leading a healthy and productive life?" The emphasis is on the word *assist*, because parents need to see their role in this manner. Parents cannot force a child to change and they should not become so involved in the problems of their child that they ignore their own lives. This is not an easy task.

## Confront the dysfunctional behaviors

Parents who make deals with the adolescent or avoid ever mentioning the subject of alcohol and drugs to the addicted teenager will be caught in a web of codependence that will leave their home a place of loneliness and bitterness.

## Define your responsibility

Parents must draw limits on their responsibility. The majority of teenagers involved with drugs or other illegal behavior will respond to treatment without the necessity of parents contacting authorities. Sometimes, however, parents must contact the authorities, if their own lives or the welfare of their family or others are threatened (for example, if the child steals the family car or drives while intoxicated). Parents usually cannot handle such a crisis by themselves.

## Confront your own addictive behaviors

Problems in the home may seem mountainous, but sometimes parents use the problems of their child to avoid the challenges of their own lives. For instance, parents who avoid their own drinking problem and focus on their teenager's drug abuse are living in a world just as unhealthy as that of the adolescent.

## Protect your marriage

Parents can easily avoid the anguish in their marital relationship by focusing on their difficult teenager as "the problem." In the long term this can be disastrous. Parents who thus ignore the dysfunction in their marriage eventually will find that once their children are grown and gone, their spouse has become a stranger.

With no child remaining on whom they may focus attention, they no longer have a scapegoat who can carry blame for the depression and arguments in the family.

### Keep your family life "normal"

Parents should not curb the life of the family because of the behavior of one child. Parents who deeply involve themselves with the "problem child" while neglecting their other children suffer the emptiness and resentment of codependence as the major dynamic of their lives.

A child who is an embarrassment at family gatherings should not stop the family from gathering. A child who refuses to go on trips or outings with the family should not stop the family from going on such outings. And parents should not keep the family at home for fear that their brief absence will cause the teenager to "get into trouble." Orbiting the family's life around the life of only one member is codependent behavior.

### Get help

Parents can find help in such dilemmas by seeking a counselor experienced with such issues. This is the most effective way of gaining help to make difficult decisions about the family and about the child with addiction problems. Parents also can join self-help groups for parents and thus receive encouragement from other parents who face similar quandaries. This is a healthy first step to solving problems in a *non*-codependent fashion.

# Do's and don'ts for parents

The following is a list of simple suggestions that can help parents struggling with the addictions of their teenager.

### Do's

1.  Do begin communicating with your teenager. It is impossible to address the issue of substance abuse if you do not even talk with each other in a reasonable fashion.

2.  Do seek a therapist or treatment program that can help your family deal with the problem of addiction. The addiction must be addressed as a family issue if the treatment is to be effective.

3. Do set limits on the activities of your child, including a prohibition of the use of drugs and alcohol (especially its use in the house).

4. Do seek help from the proper authorities if your teenager becomes violent or irresponsible (such as stealing your keys to drive the car).

5. Do work with school authorities who have experience with drug and alcohol problems.

6. Do maintain communication with your child if he runs away from home—but don't relax the limits on your responsibilities or your child's drug use. Communicate, don't bargain, to get the adolescent to come home.

7. Do continue to communicate with all family members (other children or others who live in the house) about their difficulties and don't just focus on the child with drug or alcohol problems.

8. Do address your own addiction problems. This will take courage and help from others, but you will ultimately help not only your teenager, but yourself as well.

## Don'ts

1. Don't allow your child to come and go without limits as to time or the use of alcohol or drugs in the house. People have asked me, "Why just in the house?" My answer is that you can and should show disapproval for all drug use by a child, but we have control over the presence of drugs only in the house. Parents cannot police their child night and day, but they can explain to their child the consequences of bringing drugs into the house. (Those consequences should all be negative, even to the point of contacting the police.)

2. Don't allow anger at your child's behavior to end in screaming sessions or in physical violence.

3. Don't make deals with your child that allow him to skip school, shirk homework, avoid chores, and so on, if only they stop using drugs and alcohol.

4. Don't make deals that allow the use of drugs in the house.

5.  Don't treat your child as "one of the gang" by drinking with him or by participating in any other of his dysfunctional behaviors.

6.  Don't allow your child to focus on your faulty behavior and thus switch the subject of a conversation. Admit your mistakes, then return to the subject of your child's drug use.

7.  Don't focus so intently on the child with drug problems that you disregard the lives of other family members.

8.  Don't avoid discussing the drug abuse of your child with other family members. Don't maintain the "family taboo" against mentioning the problem of drug abuse.

9.  Don't avoid your own character defects and addiction problems by convincing yourself that you can handle yours without a program or help from others.

# *Reflections*

1.  What healthy steps have you taken to address the family's problems with an addicted family member?

2.  Review the lists of do's and don'ts, and after each item, rate yourself: never, sometimes, or often. What have you discovered about yourself that you had not previously realized?

## 17

# When Does a Teenager Need Treatment?

**R**ecently, articles in magazines and newspapers have questioned the wisdom of putting teenagers into treatment programs. The writers cite examples in which a treatment experience made the teenager bitter and treatment counselors exploited the parents—desperate for help in dealing with family problems.

The articles allege that normal family conflict and standard adolescent problems have been labeled as psychiatric or chemical dependency problems needing inpatient treatment. Because people facing such problems are highly vulnerable, they easily may be exploited by professionals eager to keep the beds full in their treatment facilities.

Parents do feel helpless in making a sound judgment about these matters. If their teenager acts unruly or depressed the parents may have no idea what to do or how to discern the cause of such behavior. Yet such behavior simply may be part of the adolescent's battle of emotions.

On the other hand, there definitely are times when a teenage child may need professional help and even long-term treatment in a residential center or hospital. A trained therapist with experience in child and adolescent therapy can help parents make the right choice for treating their child's needs. Organizations such as

Tough Love (a self-help group for parents—see the list in the epilogue) also can help parents to assess the situation in their homes.

If treatment is being recommended, parents should respond with probing questions. This will help them and the professional decide what is the best option for the child and the parents. The following questions will help parents who face the possibility of admitting their adolescents to a treatment program.

# Guidelines for choosing treatment

1.  What is being recommended for our child? Although inpatient treatment is being recommended, why wouldn't residential treatment or outpatient treatment be just as helpful? How will this treatment help our teenager?

2.  What are the treatment options, and how do they compare to the one recommended for our child? Who is recommending the treatment, and what will that person gain by our accepting that option? (Therapists and physicians must be paid for their services.) In the case of our counselor, does that gain seem reasonable?

3.  Is the primary therapist admitting our child into treatment experienced and educated in child and adolescent therapy? What is her background in dealing with teenagers?

4.  What is the program of treatment in the clinic or hospital where our child will be treated? What is the daily routine my child will follow? Will school be included?

5.  Who are the staff members assisting the primary therapist in treating my child? Will I be able to talk to them about the program?

6.  What are the stages of treatment, and how will the decision be made to move our child to the next stage? How long is the average length of stay in the program and how long is the average time in each stage?

7.  How will we, the parents, be involved in the treatment process? Are there family groups? May we receive therapy for our own needs as a part of the program? May we talk to

other parents whose children have been through the program? Will those children give us candid insights on their experiences in the program? (Many of the addiction factors faced by the adolescent are parent-child issues, so the resolution of family conflicts is crucial in the recovery process for the teenager and for the whole family—especially because some family members may be codependents.)

8. What kind of continuing care will the program offer after our child has completed the program? Will we take part in this continuing care?

9. Will our child be introduced to self-help support programs during regular treatment? Is this a normal part of the program?

10. How will the decision be made that our child has completed the needed treatment and can be discharged? Will someone follow our teenager's case through continuing care? May our child use this person as a resource for further sessions of therapy when crises or major stressors enter our child's life?

11. IIow much is the cost? Will our insurance pay for this program? What are we, the parents, expected to pay?

12. Will our child be given medications during treatment? If yes, what is the purpose of these medications? What are the possible side effects? How long does the prescribing physician expect these medications to be used?

13. If our child is in a residential setting, what kind of facilities are there? May we see the facilities? With whom will my child room? How many will be in a room? Will my child have personal space for storage?

14. What are the patient rules of the program? What happens if the rules are violated?

15. What is the program policy if our child relapses? What is the treatment program for relapse, and what is the program for the prevention of relapse? Will we, as well as our child, be taught the early signs of relapse?

# Cooperating with a treatment program

The most important characteristics of people treating chemically dependent adolescents are: (1) *consistency* in their message to the adolescents; and (2) physical and emotional *availability*. The staff members of any treatment program should be continually part of the treatment team, not rotated to other programs. They should be people who practice emotional intimacy in the style of good parents; they should be people who set limits on teenage behavior; they should be warm and caring.

During treatment the adolescent should be trained in assertiveness so that she can make her own decisions, an important quality in recovery from chemical dependence. However, staff members and parents of the teenager must remember that the adolescent is not an adult and therefore needs to be supplied with alternatives from which to choose. Too much responsibility is as detrimental as a total lack of structure.

During treatment the teenager also should be encouraged to build a network of support among peers. These relationships cannot be substituted with the warmth and caring of adults.

The teenager must keep connected with what is happening to others "back at home." This includes maintaining school during treatment and allowing time for sports and other diversions. Teenagers need time to let off steam by playing basketball, swimming, listening to music, and other activities. They need this even more than adults, because they have not yet developed a long attention span. Because they have more energy than adults, they get restless and need to unleash this energy.

A treatment program should be more structured for teenagers than for adults. Teenagers need more structure and less responsibility for personal decisions than adults should have. Adult responsibility seems awesome to them and overwhelming. They have had too much of this already by choosing to use drugs and alcohol.

Now they need time to return to adolescence and enjoy a more carefree style of life. They need time to gradually grow into adult responsibility. Teenagers need a chance to *rest* so that they can grow physically, intellectually, and emotionally. Structure helps them to rest by removing responsibility from their shoulders.

# *Reflections*

1.  Have you seriously considered a treatment program for your child? What are your opinions about treatment programs?

2.  What is your greatest fear about urging your son or daughter into treatment? What is your greatest hope?

3.  Who else in your family needs a treatment program for alcoholism or drug addiction?

# *Epilogue*

I wish to close this book with a message of hope. Parents often come to therapy without such hope, but I often remember the phrase and share it with them: "Where there is life, there is hope." Parents have given life to their children and struggled to raise them. God has the power to give them hope, even when they are told that the situation is hopeless. This is the message of resurrection in the midst of death.

Parents cannot hold on to hope for very long, however, without help from others—from other parents and from professionals working in the field of addiction treatment. The following is a list of organizations to which a parent can turn. Dialing the number is the first step on the road to hope. I urge you to call today and find the help you need.

**LifeCare Christian Therapy Center: (800) PSALMS 91**

This Christian counseling therapy program has locations in cities throughout the United States. Dedicated to quality care and spiritual health, LifeCare provides inpatient and outpatient services to people of all ages.

**National Recovery Hotline: (800) 231-6946**

**National Runaway Switchboard: (800) 621-4000**

These two groups provide a national network for youth on the streets. Young people may call for help, and parents may call to attempt to contact their children. Both organizations provide referrals to programs that help young people get off the streets and into programs of recovery.

### National Youth Crisis Hotline: (800) 448-4663

This group provides phone counseling and referral services to troubled youth, as well as support programs for youth attempting to maintain a healthy lifestyle.

### Starting Point: (800) 722-5679

A quality program affiliated with Dr. Farris's work. In southern California call (714) 642-3505.

### Teen Challenge: (800) 540-4440

A program for teenagers that provides drug counseling and rehabilitation. This group works with individuals, but also in schools, prisons, and other institutions, providing youth with a way out of addiction.

### Tough Love: (800) 333-1069

A support group for parents of troubled children, members meet weekly for concrete solutions to their problems, with guest lecturers discussing the situation of addiction and codependence.

# LifeCare™ Books

LifeCare Books, the Christian imprint of CompCare Publishers, is a spirited line of innovative Christian titles based on the premise that the answers to life's deepest problems begin with biblical truth. Unequivocally Christian, psychologically valid, and backed by the solid reputation of CompCare Publishers, LifeCare Books meets the growing need for recovery and emotional health resources in a biblical context.

# The LifeCare™ Foundation

The Foundation, headquartered in Ft. Worth, Texas, seeks to help people gain wholeness in their relationships with God, self and others through the application of biblically based principles. You can reach the LifeCare Foundation by calling 800/PSALMS 91.

*LifeCare*™ **Books**
from **CompCare® Publishers**

2415 Annapolis Lane
Minneapolis, MN 55441
800/328-3330   612/559-4800
FAX 612/559-2415

# Don't Miss These Offerings from LifeCare

***Starving for Attention:*** *A young Woman's Struggle with and Triumph over Anorexia Nervosa* by Cherry Boone O'Neill. A 90's edition of Cherry Boone O'Neill's best-selling book. As the daughter of singer/actor Pat Boone, Cherry felt pressure to be the "perfect" celebrity daughter. This candid account details her battle with anorexia nervosa and her triumph over it through the love of her husband and family, and her faith in God. $13.95 Order #0-89638-274-5

***The Adam & Eve Complex:*** *Freedom from the Shame that Can Separate You from God, Others, and Yourself* by Curtis A Levang, Ph.D. In the tradition of *Telling Yourself the Truth* and *Tired of Trying to Measure Up*, Dr. Levang traces the genesis of shame back to Adam and Eve's sin in the Garden of Eden-and offers a way to heal in a gracefilled journey to recovery. $10.95 Order #0-89638-273-7

# Gift Books from CompCare

***The Love Therapy Book*** by Kathleen Keating and illustrated by Mimi Noland. Anyone can be a love therapist! This delightful new gift book proves it! From the best-selling author/illustrator team that brought the ***Hug Therapy*** books to life, ***The Love Therapy Book*** is all about love and filled with adorable dragons!
$6.95 Order #0-89638-272-9

***The Hug Therapy Book*** by Kathleen Keating and illustrated by Mimi Noland. The gift book of healthy hugs. Kathleen Keating, a psychotherapist, uses adorable hug bears to show how all kinds of hugs yield measurable, positive results on IQ, aging, self-esteem, stress, etc. $5.95 #0-89638-065-3

***Hug Therapy 2*** by Kathleen Keating and illustrated by Mimi Noland. The sequel to *The Hug Therapy Book, Hug Therapy 2* is a treasure-house of more hugs! $5.95 Order #0-89638-130-7

CompCare and **LifeCare** books are available at fine bookstores everywhere, or by calling **(800) 328-3330**. Ask for your **free** catalog!